The Aesthetics of
TONI MORRISON

SPEAKING THE UNSPEAKABLE

Edited by
Marc C. Conner

University Press of Mississippi
Jackson

To my parents

www.upress.state.ms.us

Copyright © 2000 by University Press of Mississippi
All rights reserved
Manufactured in the United States of America

08 07 06 05 04 03 02 01 00   4 3 2 1

∞

Library of Congress Cataloging-in-Publication Data

The aesthetics of Toni Morrison : speaking the unspeakable / edited and with
an introduction by Marc C. Conner.
p.   cm.
Includes bibliographical references and index.
ISBN 1-57806-284-5 (alk. paper) — ISBN 1-57806-285-3 (pbk. : alk. paper)
1. Morrison, Toni—Criticism and interpretation.   2. Afro-American aesthetics.
3. Aesthetics in literature.   4. Afro-American women in literature.
5. Narration (Rhetoric).   I. Reyes-Conner, Marc Cameron, 1963–
PS3563.O8749 Z53   2000
813'.54—dc21
00-021405

British Library Cataloging-in-Publication Data available

INTRODUCTION

Aesthetics and the African American Novel

Marc C. Conner

"For who shall describe beauty? What is it?"

W. E. B. Du Bois, "Criteria of Negro Art," 1926

"There is something irresistibly displaced and marginal about the now common and limiting phrase 'aesthetic considerations.'"

Raymond Williams, *Keywords*, 1976

"The discussion of black literature in critical terms is unfailingly sociology and almost never art criticism."

Toni Morrison, "Memory, Creation, Writing," 1984

In "The World and the Jug," Ralph Ellison's powerful meditation upon the roles of aesthetics and politics in the African-American novel, Ellison makes a key distinction: "The novel," he urges, "is *always* a public gesture, though not necessarily a political one." Few American authors have been more aware than Ellison of the unyielding connections between the work of art and life as it is lived, that is, between the aesthetic and the political realms. Indeed, Ellison insists that the African-American writer must engage "the original American ideals of social and political justice." Yet Ellison's distinction suggests that the novel, while necessarily political, is not *only* political, and those who view the novel as only a political tool reduce it to something quite other than a work of art. Such critics, Ellison asserts, "should abandon literature for politics" (Ellison, 110, 112).

Toni Morrison emerged as a major novelist in the wake of the 1960s, a decade fraught with contested ideas of the relations between the work of art and the political arena. For Morrison, the claim that art is somehow divorced from the political realm—what she has called "the art/politics fake debate" ("Preface" ix)—is absurd; like Ellison, she is committed to an art that is both aesthetically powerful and politically effective: "for me," she states, "a novel has to be socially responsible as well as very beautiful" (Jones and Vinson 183). Such a position demands a criticism that is cognizant of the political power of Morrison's writing, and also emphasizes the multiple elements of her work that belong to the domain of art. Yet despite the impressive growth in Morrison scholarship in recent years—no living American author has commanded more attention and critical production in the last two decades— there is an absence in Morrison scholarship, a silence that threatens to limit her writing and its reception. Critics consistently view her novels primarily through a political or ideological lens, thereby obscuring the specifically aesthetic elements of her work.[1] To employ Morrison's own words, quoted above, the scholarship risks partaking too much of "sociology," not enough of "art criticism."

But as the opening epigrams suggest, "the aesthetic" constitutes a contested and often ill-defined series of discourses. Recent scholarship has gone far in dismissing the myth of an isolated, "apolitical" aesthetic realm—what Terry Eagleton terms the "disabling idea of aesthetic autonomy" (9; see also Jay, "'The Aesthetic Ideology'" 71–83). Yet the contrary impulse, to see the aesthetic as only a reflection or expression of political ideology, is equally crippling, and has dominated criticism in the last three decades. As George Levine argues, the aesthetics/politics struggle "has led to a reductive assimilation of literature to ideology or to a resistant sense that the literary and the political should have nothing to do with each other." Subsuming the aesthetic to the political, or making the cleavage between them absolute, simultaneously refuses to see the potentially liberating effects of art, and obscures the real fact that the specifically aesthetic realm "operates differently from others and contributes in distinctive ways to the possibilities of human fulfillment and connection." Thus Levine asserts that "no criticism that refuses distinctions between aesthetic and instrumental functions of language can do justice either to the aesthetic or the ideological" (1, 3, 9).

Indeed, the aesthetic domain has always approached the work of art in both its internal aspects, or qualities of form, and its external aspects, or qualities of content. The category of "the aesthetic," over the course of its long existence, concerns itself with two primary elements: the effect of the work of art on the perceiver, and the work of art in and of itself, without consideration of external elements. The idea of readerly "affect"—Aristotle's catharsis, Horace's delight, Longinus's sublime, Kant's disinterested contemplation, Gadamer's hermenuetic circle—has long been central to aesthetic study. Similarly, the idea that the work of art demands an analysis devoted only to its internal form and structure—what M. H. Abrams terms the "art-as-such" position (135)—still retains its power today as an effort to focus solely upon the art work itself. Clearly these almost contrary impulses of the aesthetic, its "ostensibly paradoxical efforts toward disinterest and community" (Levine 25), suggest that aesthetic analysis has always looked both outside of the work of art, to the domain of the audience, and within the work of art, to its formal constituents. To return to Ellison's formulation, aesthetic analysis is both public and private, external and internal.

Toni Morrison's writing emerges from a complex array of aesthetic and cultural traditions, yet the overwhelming tendency in Morrison scholarship—a tendency fostered by Morrison herself—has been to ignore or even to deny diverse influences. The great anxiety in Morrison scholarship, and unquestionably in Morrison's own critical writings, is the question of originality, of indebtedness. As Morrison herself has famously stated, "I am not *like* James Joyce; I am not *like* Thomas Hardy; I am not *like* Faulkner. . . . my effort is to be *like* something that has probably only been fully expressed in music" (McKay, "An Interview" 152). Morrison laments the effort of critics to "place [her work] into an already established literary tradition." "I find such criticism dishonest," she asserts, "because it never goes into the work on its own terms. It comes from some other place and finds content outside of the work and wholly irrelevant to it" (Tate 161). Morrison desires an aesthetic analysis, but one that will reveal only her immersion in what she terms "Black style," a style that she asserts will "faithfully. . . reflect the aesthetic tradition of Afro-American culture" (Wilson 136, Morrison, "Memory" 388–89).

The scholarship detailing Morrison's position within a specifically African-American aesthetic and cultural tradition is vast and impressive,[2] and certainly an understanding of Morrison's work requires immersion in "ways of knowing," to borrow Nellie McKay's phrase ("Introduction" 3), that are not necessarily a part of the western tradition: African and African-American myth and language, African-American musical traditions of the spirituals, blues, and jazz, alternative approaches to history, religion, and ancestry, culture-specific concepts and philosophical ideas of time and cosmology that are often opposed to traditional western concepts, and many more. However, this emphasis in Morrison scholarship is blind to Morrison's positions within a more diverse aesthetic tradition. In her introduction to the *Critical Essays on Toni Morrison*, McKay states that Morrison's novels "are a rejection of white patriarchal modernism," yet two paragraphs later McKay adds, as if in an afterthought, that "as a teenager, Morrison read the European literary masters—English, Russian, and French" ("Introduction" 2–3). There is no attempt to reconcile these apparently contrary positions, nor any attempt to account for Morrison's master's thesis on Faulkner and Woolf, high modernists to be sure, nor her formal training in Classics at Howard University.[3] It is as if, in their zeal to bring into relief the specifically African-American elements of Morrison's writing, critics have turned a blind eye to the clear presence of other elements in that writing. Yet this is precisely to deny some of the most astonishing and enlightening features of Morrison's work; and it results in only a partial view of her literary achievement.

Indeed, Morrison herself has suggested that any critical view that would blind itself to her training in a western, even classical background is misguided. She has stated that her awareness of "the consciousness of being black" did not begin for her until she left Cornell and began teaching in the late 1950s, when she was nearly thirty: "I came to [the value of being black] as a clear statement very late in life, I think, because I left home . . . and went to school, and the things I studied were Western and, you know, I was terrifically fascinated with all of that, and at that time any information that came to me from my own people seemed to me to be backwoodsy and uninformed. You know, they hadn't read all these wonderful books" (Jones and Vinson 173–74). In the meantime she had studied Latin for four years, taken degrees in classics and literature, and written a Master's Thesis that employed structures of Greek Tragedy to understand the work of Faulkner and Woolf. Consequently, it seems indisputable that her engagement with a western, classical tradition preceded her engagement with a *literary* African-American tradition.[4] The classical tradition has influenced the writing of all her major novels, as suggested by her comments that "the Greek chorus . . . reminds me of what goes on in Black churches and in jazz," and that the *denoument* of many of her novels "is Greek" in its sense of "suffering" and "realization" (Jones and Vinson 176–77). And though Morrison has cautioned against the use of

apostle of Truth and Right not by choice but *by inner and outer compulsion.*
Free he is but *his freedom is ever bounded* by Truth and Justice; and slavery
only dogs him when he is denied the right to tell the Truth or recognize an
ideal of Justice." "Thus," he famously concludes, "all Art is propaganda and
ever must be. . . . I do not care a damn for any art that is not used for propaganda" (999, emphasis added). Du Bois's position is certainly defendable,
committed as he was to social betterment for a bitterly oppressed people; yet
his link between beauty and "compulsion," and his insistence that African-
American art must be "propaganda," is surely troubling. This same tension
between constraint and liberty is stated in Langston Hughes's landmark essay, "The Negro Artist and the Racial Mountain," published the same year
as Du Bois's essay. Hughes argues that there is no such thing as an African-
American poet who is simply a "poet," independent of race—such a poet is
really "a white poet." Hughes asserts that the effort to be anything other than
a certain kind of "black" in one's poetry is the cause for "shame": "So I am
ashamed for the black poet who says, 'I want to be a poet, not a Negro poet'"
(692–94). Thus, like Du Bois, Hughes offers condemnation to any artist who
seeks an aesthetic independent of Hughes's idea of racial authenticity.

This sort of program of constraint and conformity shapes the political-
aesthetic debate in African-American writing in the decades to follow, most
prominently in Richard Wright's influential "Blueprint for Negro Writing"
of 1937. The essay's very title suggests that the African-American novel
ought to follow a certain fixed form, which for Wright consists of a narrow
Marxist-naturalist design that would create "a unified sense of a common life
and a common fate" which, when properly understood by an African-American writer, "should unify his personality, organize his emotions, buttress him
with a tense and obdurate will to change the world" (59–60). As with Du
Bois and Hughes, Wright's goal is to bring about positive social change; yet
the terms he employs in this essay—molding the consciousness, unifying,
organizing, making common—all suggest the troubling emphasis on unity,
conformity, and constraint evident in Du Bois and Hughes. And as with those
earlier writers, to be opposed to this blueprint is to be an outcast.

Such was precisely the position of Zora Neale Hurston. No writer in the
African-American tradition is more committed to the freedom of the artist
than Hurston. In her lively essay of 1928, "How It Feels to Be Colored Me,"
Hurston takes up the challenge of being simultaneously black and a writer in
a way that explicitly rebukes the constraint put forth by Hughes just two

years before. "I am not tragically colored," she asserts. "There is no great sorrow dammed up in my soul, nor lurking behind my eyes. . . . I do not belong to the sobbing school of Negrohood who hold that nature somehow has given them a lowdown dirty deal and whose feelings are all hurt about it" (215–16). Hurston insists that race is neither a constraint nor a burden to the artist—a bold aesthetic statement, given the climate of conformity that surrounded her. She lived and wrote in this fashion, and she paid the price.

Hurston's famous split with Hughes over the composition of *Mule Bone* in 1930–1931 may have been a symptom of the aesthetic and political differences between them; Hurston called it "the great cross of her life," and her sense of betrayal certainly began taking shape at this time.[5] Soon after her split with Hughes, the most scathing denunciation of Hurston's writing came from Wright, who wrote of *Their Eyes Were Watching God* that the novel had no "basic idea or theme that lends itself to significant interpretation. . . . The sensory sweep of her novel carries no theme, no message, no thought" ("Between Laughter"). Wright's review was echoed by Alain Locke, supposedly one of Hurston's closest friends during the Harlem Renaissance, who similarly complained that Hurston needed to "come to grips with motive fiction and social document fiction" (Hemenway 241). The complaint leveled against Hurston was a political one—that she is insufficiently engaged in the social-political struggles of her day—masked in aesthetic terms.[6] After her condemnation for the alleged "immoral act" in 1948, Hurston blamed her own people for her fall. Despite an utter lack of evidence, the African-American press published several sensational, condemning articles, prompting Hurston's now-famous lament: "My race has seen fit to destroy me without reason, and with the vilest tools conceived of by man so far. . . . All that I have ever tried to do has proved useless. All that I have believed in has failed me. . . . I feel hurled down a filthy privy hole" (Hemenway 321–22). The connection between her independent views on art and politics and her condemnation are provocative, particularly in the light of Hughes's private glee over her fall.[7] Hurston's life reflects the pariah status foisted upon the African-American artist who refused to conform her work or her life to any "blueprint," and her fate explains her statement that "race consciousness is a deadly explosive on the tongues of men" (quoted in Gates, "Writing 'Race'" 5).

In this respect—and in many others—Ellison is the heir to Hurston. His most pronounced and forceful aesthetic statements, made in the early 1960s well after the astonishing success of *Invisible Man,* came in response to Wright's theories; here Ellison made his crucial distinction that novels, while always public gestures, are not necessarily political ones. Rather than being a tool for mere social protest—to Ellison the most elementary form of writing—Ellison sees the novel as a creative form that is as rich as its possibilities are allowed to be: "Wright believed in the much abused idea that novels are 'weapons'—the counterpart of the dreary notion, common among most minority groups, that novels are instruments of good public relations. But I believe that true novels, even when most pessimistic and bitter, arise out of an impulse to celebrate human life and therefore are ritualistic and ceremonial at their core. Thus they would preserve as they destroy, affirm as they reject." Ellison concludes by stating—in a formula that reads like a reply to Du Bois's famous dictum about art and propaganda—that "the inadequacy characteristic of most novels by Negroes [is] simple failure of craft . . . *the desire to have protest perform the difficult tasks of art*" (114, 137, emphasis added). For Ellison, the novel, while being inescapably and necessarily political, is principally a matter of aesthetics. Any other position would limit and constrict that art.

Despite the overwhelmingly positive reviews of *Invisible Man*, the African-American left criticized the novel's failure to address the social ills of African-Americans (Busby 117). These negative views were repeated in Irving Howe's well-known critique of Ellison for being insufficiently protest-oriented, and for "the sudden, unprepared and implausible assertion of unconditioned freedom" in *Invisible Man* (Howe 115). But the most telling critiques of Ellison emerged in the 1960s, when Ellison grew increasingly opposed—particularly on the crucial question of the relations between art and politics—to the Black Power and Black Aesthetic movements that dominated African-American intellectual and cultural life. Ellison's avowedly "integrative" approach to art clashed with the increasingly "separatist" position of many African-American intellectuals in that decade, and the intolerance of the Black Aesthetic enhanced Ellison's opposition to the ideal of a separate and independent Black Art. As a consequence, at Oberlin in 1969 Ellison was nearly booed off the stage by black students, one of whom shouted that he was an "Uncle Tom" (O'Meally, "Ralph Ellison" 247; see also Walling). Ellison's famous literary silencing may well have been related to the atmosphere of intolerance and constraint that surrounded his life after *Invisible Man*.

The Black Aesthetic movement is the third stage, after the Harlem Renaissance and the debates of mid-century, in this formidable theorizing about the relationship between art and politics in African-American writing. The Black Aesthetic subsumes "aesthetics" beneath politics (Gayle, "Introduction" xvii-xviii, xxi; Fuller 3), and adheres to the blueprint of constraint, for its three great predecessors were precisely Du Bois, Hughes, and Wright, and its great opponent within African-American culture was Ellison.[8] Addison Gayle's conclusion to his landmark anthology *The Black Aesthetic* uses Hughes's arguments to dismiss the work of prominent African-American writers whom he sees as "literary assimilationists," among whom he includes James Weldon Johnson, James Baldwin, and Ralph Ellison ("The Function of Literature" 407, 411). Such exclusion of three of the most prominent African-American writers prompts Houston Baker's awareness of the shortcomings of the Black Aesthetic — its tendencies toward "chauvinism," "cultural xenophobia," and its lack of a "distinctive theoretical vocabulary" ("Generational Shifts" 296, 301) — and explains his claim that the Black Aesthetic, however understandable and even inevitable, was "probably not the most fruitful approach to the black literary text" (*The Journey Back* xii).

And yet, to dismiss the efforts of the Black Aesthetic movement out of hand is a suspect and facile gesture, and quite contrary to the impulses of the present volume. For despite its apparent rejection of traditional aesthetic concepts, the Black Aesthetic movement offers a thoughtful and critical *engagement* with traditional aesthetics that reveals much about both aesthetics and the African-American novel. "The Black Arts Movement," asserts Larry Neal, "proposes a radical reordering of the Western cultural aesthetic," particularly its absolute exclusion of all aspects relevant to African-American life, and its desire to conceal its own political ideology beneath the innocent facade of art (273). As Gayle argues, the "western aesthetic" has always implicitly devalued the concerns of cultural others, and has written into its critical positions certain political values and judgements: "The white aesthetic, despite the academic critics, has always been with us. . . . the poets of biblical times were discussing beauty in terms of light and dark — the essential characteristics of a white and black aesthetic — and establishing the dichotomy of superior vs. inferior which would assume body and form in the 18th century" ("Cultural Strangulation" 40). These criticisms of the western aesthetic tradition — and the larger western cultural tradition of which aesthetics form such a crucial part — are quite familiar to us today: hardly color-blind, this tradition is all too aware of the distinctions of color; hardly apolitical, this tradition is rife with political implications and consequences; hardly universal, this tradition emerges from—and speaks for—a particular cultural constituency, and its claims to universality are part of its will to power. At its best, the Black Aesthetic movement sought to call the hegemony of the western aesthetic tradition into question, to reveal its limitations and its weaknesses, and to show where African Americans and African-American cultural practice depart from and contest with this tradition. Its primary aim was, as Cheryl Wall has argued, "toward an ideal where ethics and aesthetics were one" (287).

Critical discourse in the decades following the sixties has continued the split between aesthetics and politics that has dominated African-American critical thought throughout this century. Continuing the limiting view championed by Du Bois, Hughes, Wright, and a certain strain of the Black Aesthetic, Houston Baker argues that the only valid critical practice is one that focuses exclusively on "the material bases of the society that provided the enabling conditions" for the production of literature ("Generational Shifts" 311)—what Henry Louis Gates, Jr., will describe as "race and superstructure" criticism ("Preface to Blackness" 245; indeed, Baker calls his own approach to literature "racial poetics" ([*Afro-American Poetics* 5]). Baker praises what he sees as the essential thrust of the Black Aesthetic movement: its refusal to separate "the language of criticism from the vocabulary of political ideology" ("Generational Shifts" 302), and he has called for the current generation of literary scholars to "set an agenda for Afro-American literary studies" that will focus solely on the "social," "political," and "ideological" aspects of literature ("Introduction" 1). Baker equates the literary work with political ideology, and he criticizes scholars such as Gates and Robert Stepto who do not follow this reductive formula, calling them "reconstructionists" (a caustic term to apply to African-American scholars) "who have adopted postures, standards, and vocabularies of their white compeers" ("Generational Shifts" 302–3). Such an approach is strikingly reminiscent of the "shame" Hughes claimed to feel for the poet who does not adhere to Hughes's narrow notion of racial authenticity, and not far from the "Uncle Tom" charge leveled at Ellison in the 1960s.

Stepto, in contrast, describes such ideology-driven approaches to the literary work of art as "nonreading," a practice that "encourages ingenious manipulation of *nonliterary structures* instead of immersion in the multiple images and landscapes of metaphor" ("The Reconstruction" 15, emphasis added)— that is, a refusal to engage the text on its own terms and in its own language.

Similarly, Gates points out that the tendency to view African-American literature through a largely political lens has caused "the structure of the black text [to be] *repressed* and treated as if it were transparent"; the text has become "the very thing *not* to be explained, as if it were invisible, or literal, or a one-dimensional document." Gates and Stepto recognize that the political approach to African-American literature has reduced that literature, constraining its imaginative, symbolic, and mythic possibilities to fit a narrow ideological straightjacket. What is needed instead, Gates argues, is "the sorts of theories concerned with discrete uses of figurative language" ("Criticism in the Jungle" 5–6) — precisely the domain of traditional aesthetics, and the avenue for exploring the work's aesthetic *and* political power. For, as Valerie Smith has stated, "we can discern [literature's] politics and its relation to ideology only through close analysis of its language" (7).

Often, as the preceding arguments illustrate, "the political" in African-American discourse becomes synonymous with "race": to write an authentically "black" literature, the essence of the work must be of a particular political thrust. Hence to seek or create an artistic content that is not dependent upon race becomes anti-political (this is Hughes's argument in "The Negro Artist"). The result of this identification of the political with the racial is to reduce both categories to mere formulae, and to resist the complexity both of the political reality and of racial questions within the African-American community itself. As Morrison herself insists, black art cannot be reduced to mere "sociology" — its reality is too complex and rich for such reduction. Furthermore, the difficulty of art vs. politics is particularly pressing in the case of African-American literature because, as Gates points out, that literature has always descended from two traditions, has always been "double-voiced": "In the case of the writer of African descent, her or his texts occupy spaces in at least two traditions: a European or American literary tradition, and one of the several related but distinct black traditions. The 'heritage' of each black text written in a Western language is, then, a double heritage" ("Criticism in the Jungle" 4) — another consequence of what Du Bois has famously called the "double-consciousness" required of every African-American.

The double-voicedness of the African-American text consequently requires that African-American writing be approached in a similarly doubled manner, one that is cognizant both of the specifically African features of the writing, but also the western, or Anglo-European, features of that writing. Only such a doubled vision is capable of perceiving, and interpreting, the manner in which the text moves between the two traditions. For, as Gates points out in so much of his work, the African-American text certainly cannot be assimilated into a wholly western critical approach; rather, "black formal repetition always repeats with a difference, a black difference that manifests itself in specific language use" (*Signifying Monkey* xxii-iii). Consequently, when we approach the African-American text from the perspective of western aesthetics, we must attend to how the literature signifies upon and transforms our sense of the aesthetic tradition, and at the same time how the aesthetic tradition opens up the richness of the African-American literary work. As Gates argues, "the 'application' of a mode of reading to explicate a black text *changes both the received theory and received ideas about the text.* When this occurs, the results are 'original'" ("Criticism in the Jungle" 4, 9, emphasis added).

The bulk of Morrison scholarship views her writing in the context of political and racial ideology; the aesthetic dimensions of her work are limited to an African cosmology and an African aesthetic, which is seen as different from, if not opposed to, a western aesthetic, traditionally understood. Again, Morrison's work is certainly immersed in these fundamental African-American elements, but this is only a part of Morrison's literary universe. It is similarly indisputable that the classical aesthetic tradition played a powerful part in the formation of her mind and her imagination, and any attempt to omit this influence leads to a partial and weakened understanding of her writings. But curiously, few critics have paid attention to Morrison's training in the aesthetic tradition, and the effect of this tradition upon her writing.[9] The essays in this volume seek to right this imbalance; at the same time they seek to uncover what Morrison's work can teach us about these aesthetic traditions themselves, whether western, African, African-American, or some even more elusive category. But these essays also seek to avoid the tired oppositions that have persistently defined African-American cultural theory: Du Bois vs. Washington, Hughes vs. Hurston, Wright vs. Ellison, et cetera. The stance of opposition and rejection—certainly the most elementary of critical responses—has been all too easy in recent decades, and has led to the impoverishment of intelligent aesthetic response to the work of any number of powerful writers. Among these writers is certainly Toni Morrison, and her own position within the tradition of African-American literature makes her in many ways the most potent figure in this century-long argument about the relative importance of aesthetics in the African-American novel.

Morrison has occupied a prominent and complex position within these debates for three decades. When *The Black Aesthetic* appeared in 1971, Morrison wrote the review for *The New York Times Book Review,* praising the book's "ethical quarrel with Western culture," a culture Morrison described as "invalid, unethical, inhumane" (*Amistad 2* 34). When asked about the art-politics relation in the light of the 1960s, Morrison has stated—in words remarkably similar to those of Du Bois—that "that's what an artist is—a politician" ("Conversation" 4). Morrison definitely sees the writer's mission as politically involved: to "bear witness or effect change . . . take cataracts off people's eyes . . . enlighten and . . . strengthen" (Jones and Vinson 183). Her greatest complaint about efforts to understand her writing is the failure to comprehend her own cultural specificity: "I have yet to read criticism that understands my work or is prepared to understand it," she comments, "because [the critics] don't always evolve out of the culture, the world, the given quality out of which I write" (LeClair 128, McKay, "An Interview" 151). Thus, like Du Bois, Hughes, Wright, and their followers, she often equates her writing with a particular racial and political ideology. Similarly, intolerance and constraint appear in Morrison's work: witness her insistence in the Nobel Prize lecture that what she terms "oppressive language"—defined by Morrison as "sexist language, racist language, theistic language"—"must be rejected, altered, and exposed" (*Nobel Lecture* 9). Of course, the dangers of hate speech are powerfully clear in the late twentieth century; yet this call for the policing of language, particularly when seen in the context of a century-long struggle in the African-American tradition over precisely this question, is troubling. One wonders which writers Morrison would silence, for which writers she would feel "shame."

However, this is only one part of Morrison's views on aesthetics and liberty of expression. She resists reducing the writer's role to a purely social one. Her work, she states, "should not even attempt to solve social problems, but it should certainly try to clarify them" ("Memory" 389). "First of all," she claims in another interview, "no one should tell any writer what to write, at all, ever. . . . one of the goals of the whole business of liberation was to make it possible for us not to be silenced, no matter what we said" (E. Washington 237). And when asked by an interviewer whether the primary role of the novel is "to illuminate social reality" or "to stretch our imagination," she responded, "The latter. It really is about stretching"; "But," she then cautioned, "in that way you have to bear witness to what *is*" (Moyers 272–73). Furthermore, Morrison insists that her writing is not limited to a single culture, that—if it is truly great literature—it has a universal appeal and accessibility: "If I could understand [my writing], then I assumed two things: (a) that other Black people could understand it and (b) that white people, if it was any good, would understand it also" (Bakerman 38, Tate 160). Thus Morrison's view of the vocation of the African-American writer shifts between the two poles of the art/politics debate—her position is double-voiced, just as the African-American tradition has been throughout this century: it has a cultural specificity that resists interpretation outside of that culture; and yet it has a universality that speaks to all people.

Similarly, Morrison's statements about her own particular aesthetic status reveal a dual attitude toward these questions. On the one hand, Morrison insists that her goal is "to write literature that was irrevocably, indisputably Black," that "took as its creative task and sought as its credentials those recognized and verifiable principles of Black art" ("Memory" 389). But at the same time, her explanation of what these "principles" are reveals a vision of the aesthetic that is not limited to racial and political ideology. Though Morrison resists clarifying what precisely these "principles" are, her increasingly voluminous critical writings do reveal four main elements that seem to constitute the essence of "black" writing for her: the presence of displacement or alienation; a close relationship between author and reader; an oral quality to the voice of the text; and, at the formal level, a quality of music in the writing that is distinctively Black. When these elements come together in the work of art, they produce Morrison's own aesthetic ideal.

In her Thesis on Woolf and Faulkner, Morrison states that "alienation is a definition of this century" (1–2), and each of her novels is a meditation on alienation in the African-American world: *The Bluest Eye,* with its focus on Pecola's tragic outsider status in her own community; *Sula,* whose title character is the quintessential pariah in Morrison's work; *Song of Solomon,* in which Milkman is alienated from his family, his town, even his own ancestral past; the utter isolation between each character in *Tar Baby* (which ends with Jadine and Son still locked in their respective worlds); *Beloved*'s pervasive alienation, most movingly in Paul D's poignant astonishment at "the beauty of this land that was not his" (268); the isolation that drives Joe Trace to murder and Violet to madness in *Jazz; Paradise*'s chronicle of an African-

American group cast out from every human connection except its own increasingly insular community; and even the Nobel speech, which begins with the young people asking perhaps the definitive Morrison question: "Tell us," they demand, "what moves at the margin. What it is to have no home in this place. To be set adrift from the one you knew. What it is to live at the edge of towns that cannot bear your company" (*Nobel Lecture* 13). Morrison's novels seek to resolve this alienation, or least to learn to live with it in some measure of harmony and peace.

Morrison claims that writing is "a craft that appears solitary but needs another for its completion" (*The Dancing Mind* 14). This reader-response element that pervades Morrison's writing responds to its omnipresent alienation. "One of the major characteristics of black literature," she asserts, "is the participation of the *other*, that is, the audience, the reader." To Morrison, this is not only the hallmark of her writing, but the very function of literature: "My writing expects, demands participatory reading, and that I think is what literature is supposed to do. It's not just about telling the story; it's about involving the reader" (Christina Davis 231, Tate 164). She desires an intimacy between artist and reader that can overcome the alienation that pervades the text. Such a participatory, intimate moment is achieved in the closing moments of *Jazz*, when at the end of such a brutal and rending story the tale-teller and the reader seem to be holding one another's hands in amity and harmony (229); similarly, the final words in the Nobel speech show the old woman and the young overcoming their alienation and achieving communion: "Look," the old woman concludes—in a sentence that could stand for Morrison's entire project—"how lovely it is, this thing we have done—together" (*Nobel Lecture* 13).

Morrison ascribes both the experience of alienation and the importance of reader response to "a cultural specificity that is Afro-American" ("Unspeakable Things" 19), but certainly these categories are present throughout the canon of western literature, and the tradition of aesthetics certainly has much to say about these crucial concepts in Morrison's writing. The sublime, for example, describes the experience of alienation *par excellence*, alienation from earthly existence itself; and both the sublime and the beautiful are defined in terms of affect, the reader's response to experience. Similarly, Morrison argues that the most definitively "black" element in her work is her use of language. "It has always seemed to me that black people's grace has been with what they do with language," she has said, and she describes her writing as an attempt to "clean" and "reclaim" that language: "I try to clean the language up and give words back their original meaning, not the one that's sabotaged by constant use" (Watkins 45, Tate 165). For Morrison, this means restoring the "oral quality" of the language, and making it imitate as closely as possible "the one other art form in which black people have always excelled and that is music" (Tate 166, Stepto, "Intimate Things" 28). These oral, aural, and musical elements are intimately tied to Morrison's African-American heritage; yet they demand a broader aesthetic reading as well. For example, although the uses of jazz music in *Jazz* have much to do with the African-American musical forms and traditions current in Harlem of the 1920s, nevertheless, as I have argued elsewhere, this is only a part of that novel's structure, and probably the most obvious and least revealing part. For *Jazz* "is a densely *written* work, wrought with extreme complexity and interweaving elements, probably more comparable to a classical prelude and fugue than to the improvisatory, unstable quality of true jazz music" (Conner, "Wild Women" 354). Morrison's work is double-voiced in its aesthetic and cultural constituents, and the successful critic must demonstrate similar range.

The Joycean ideal of the artist — indifferent, invisible, paring his fingernails above the art work with no concern for its reception or its effect — is anathema to Toni Morrison. She is deeply concerned with the influence of her work upon the world at large, and she has certain hopes, if not intentions, for what that work will accomplish in the political realm. As she has described her effort, "my mode of writing is sublimely didactic" (Koenen 74). Morrison's hope is simultaneously to reveal and to heal, to strip away the illusions to show why African-American life remains to many an embattled existence, and to minister to a beleaguered population: "There has to be a mode to do what the music did for blacks, what we used to be able to do with each other in private and in that civilization that existed underneath the white civilization. I think this accounts for the address of my books. I am not explaining anything to anybody. My work bears witness and suggests who the outlaws were, who survived under what circumstances and why, what was legal in the community as opposed to what was legal outside it. All that is in the fabric of the story in order to do what the music used to do" (LeClair 120–21). The writing is uncompromisingly political; but its aspiration is to the status of art, the realm of story and music and restoration.

When Morrison speaks of "the advising, benevolent, protective, wise Black ancestor," the "matrix" of yearning and source of healing for the African-American ("City Limits, Village Values" 39), she is clearly expressing an ideal toward which she herself aspires. She gives shape to this idea in her Nobel Lecture: when the disenchanted, angry youth come to the wise old woman for guidance, she responds with story. Such is the response of Toni Morrison to late twentieth-century America and its numerous ills, racial or otherwise: the wonder of story, the grace of language. Morrison's own aesthetic vision reflects much of the foundational suppositions of the present volume: the work of art is expansive, creative, even wondrous precisely in its multifaceted power, its ability to leap the impasse of either/or and to find, even to create, new sites for feeling, thought, and action. As the wise old woman muses in the Nobel lecture, "word-work is sublime because it is generative: it makes meaning that secures our difference, our human difference" (*Nobel Lecture* 11).

The essays in this volume seek to address and engage the multiple elements that comprise Toni Morrison's art. The first essay puts into question the very concept of aesthetic thought, as Barbara Johnson examines the curious words "aesthetic" and "rapport" in *Sula*, and shows how Freud's concept of the uncanny—the psychoanalytic rendering of the Kantian sublime—explains the simultaneously "lost" and yet "familiar" character of much of Morrison's writing. Johnson's conclusion—that in *Sula* Morrison "shows that it is not a matter of choosing between politics and aesthetics, but of recognizing the profoundly political nature of the inescapability of the aesthetic within personal, political, and historical life"—could well stand as an epigram to this entire volume. The second essay suggests the ways in which traditional aesthetic concepts and African-American aesthetics overlap and contest in Morrison's work: Yvonne Atkinson reveals how Black English and the oral tradition create meaning between the text and the reader in Morrison's writing, forming a complex symmetry between the oral and the written systems to allow the reader to participate in the storytelling event.

Three essays follow that each employ aesthetic concepts long current in western philosophical practice. Susan Corey uses the category of the grotesque to examine the multiple versions of a disrupted reality in *Beloved*, and argues that Morrison uses the grotesque in both its positive and negative dimensions to expand the limits of the mysterious. The effect of this disruption is a simultaneous confrontation with and judgment upon the reader, ineluctably implicated in the harrowing tale of the novel. My own essay takes up two of the more ancient and powerful aesthetic concepts in the classical tradition, the beautiful and the sublime, and shows their role in Morrison's writing—particularly *The Bluest Eye*, *Song of Solomon*, and *Beloved*—in simultaneously constituting and indicting the relationship between the community and the individual that is so central to Morrison's work. Katherine Stern investigates the concept of beauty as both a physical idea and a philosophical category in the entire range of Morrison's writings. She argues that Morrison simultaneously rejects physical beauty as a pernicious and destructive idea, while offering an alternative approach to beauty that is "tangible and improvisational, relational and contextual, involving mutual efforts to feel as well as see." Such a recasting of beauty is both an aesthetic and an ethical gesture.

Maria DiBattista's essay complicates Morrison's very status as novelist, by examining the distinctions between the novelist and the storyteller and asking how successfully Morrison moves between these roles. The implications of this distinction for history, myth, Morrison's own life, and her project as novelist and storyteller are discussed in evocative detail. Michael Wood follows with an analysis of *Paradise* in which he examines Morrison's attraction to indeterminacy and elusive narration, and shows how this reflects her precarious status as a writer involved in a multitude of cultural and philosophical traditions. Finally, in a true piece of reader-response criticism, Cheryl Lester offers a deeply personal reading of Morrison's Nobel Prize speech and shows how its curious use of fable is linked to an aesthetic impulse that is, in the end, fundamentally concerned with the relations between the aesthetic and the ethical realms.

The hope of this volume is first to offer a number of challenging and original readings of Morrison's novels that serve to expand the ways in which those novels are read. A second hope is to show the relevance—indeed, the necessity—of a critical approach that is broad in its scope and inclusive in its aims, an approach that is cognizant of new methodologies and the splendors of a culturally vibrant critical practice, but at the same time insists upon the essential function of a long-standing and energetic tradition of the aesthetic that is powerfully present in contemporary letters. And finally this volume seeks to open up the discourse of current literary criticism, a discourse that risks growing increasingly narrow, specialized, and territorial. If these essays demonstrate anything, it is the extraordinary richness offered by the aesthetic approach to the literary work, both in terms of what this approach teaches us about the work, and what the work teaches us about an ancient but ever-changing tradition of thought and feeling that accounts for much of the power involved in the literary experience.

NOTES

1. A survey of the book-length studies treating Morrison's writing reveals an array of critical positions and theoretical approaches: Trudier Harris has examined Morrison's novels in the context of Morrison's uses of African-American folklore, arguing that Morrison both takes up traditional folk sources and at the same time transforms them into a new, "'literary' folklore" of her own (7); Denise Heinze interprets Morrison's writings as a working-out of Du Bois's famous trope of "double consciousness," arguing that Morrison creates a "double vision" that "establishes a diverse readership that crosses racial, cultural, and class lines" (11); Philip Page studies the novels through the theme of identity as both unity and multiplicity, or "fusion and fragmentation" (3); and most recently Nancy Peterson's volume of essays looks at Morrison's work from the multiple perspectives of contemporary critical theory, what Peterson terms "various theories of the post- that have come to proliferate at the end of the twentieth century in America" ("Introduction" 1).

2. See, for example, Harris's *Fiction and Folklore*, which approaches Morrison's work in terms of its use of primarily African-American folklore. Even when the folk form Morrison uses is traditionally "western," as in the appropriations of Snow White and Sleeping Beauty in *Tar Baby*, Morrison "rewrites" and "reclaims" the form "from its distortions . . . and relocates it in its Indian and African bases" (13). See also Jacqueline de Weever's study of Morrison and other African-American women writers. Essays abound that analyze Morrison's use of African and African-American elements in her fiction: see in particular Clark; Stein; Wegs; James Coleman; Lewis; Rosenberg; McDowell; Powell; Trace; and Mbalia.

3. For an outstanding argument for Morrison's indebtedness to a tradition other than a solely African-American one, see Cowart, who argues persuasively that Morrison is "a novelist whose Afro-American sensibility [is] overdetermined," and whose indebtedness to Faulkner and Joyce in particular is unmistakable and, curiously, only "briefly noted" in "passing references" by most Morrison critics (87, 89). See also Kolmerton, Ross, and Wittenberg, who note "Morrison's complexly ambiguous response to the Faulknerian heritage, which oscillates between admiration and intense ambivalence" (xi); and Duvall.

4. This is further confirmed by Morrison's statement that she had not even read Zora Neale Hurston, with the exception of one short story, when she began writing her first novel (Naylor 214). This comment implies that McKay's observation that Morrison's "artistic precursors" are Phillis Wheatley, Jessie Fauset, and Hurston must be true only in a broad literary-historical sense, hardly in a sense of direct influence (McKay, "An Interview," 138).

5. On the mysterious *Mule Bone* incident, see Hemenway, 136–48; Rampersad, 184–85, 193–98; and Hughes's own, rather selective, version in his *The Big Sea*, 311–34.

6. Wright's critique may likely have come in response to Hurston's public rejection of Wright's aesthetic — which she characterized as "pitiful" and "the solution of the PARTY" — in her review of Wright's *Uncle Tom's Children* (quoted in Hemenway, 334–35). For a particularly fine discussion of Hurston's differences, aesthetically and politically, from Wright, see Washington and Wall.

7. Rampersad reports that Hughes "had giggled to Arna Bontemps about her predicament" when he heard the news of her scandal; Hughes did agree, upon subpoena, to testify on behalf of Hurston's character in the scheduled trial, though he confessed to being "amazed" at the request, since he and Hurston had never reconciled after the *Mule Bone* incident (Rampersad, *The Life of Langston Hughes, Volume II*: 163–64).

8. In his introduction to *The Black Aesthetic*, Gayle calls Du Bois "the old master," and claims that Wright and Hughes epitomize the movement, whereas the position of Ellison — who insisted that "blacks are not an African people but an American one" — is anathema to an authentic Black Aesthetic (xxii). As one critic has argued, "Ellison's is the achievement that . . . Gayle must reject when he wishes to replace a complex and perhaps perverse heritage with a simple art of straightforward expression and black pieties" (Charles Davis 103).

9. Studies that have taken classical aesthetic concepts into account in an analysis of Morrison's work include Byerman and Bowers; Peterson's *Toni Morrison: Critical and Theoretical Approaches*, while not explicitly associated with classical aesthetics, certainly crosses over into this terrain, as much contemporary theory does. For a fine discussion of the tensions between Morrison's "aesthetic" and traditional aesthetics, see the opening chapter of Heinze's *The Dilemma of Double Consciousness*.

The Aesthetics of

TONI
MORRISON

"AESTHETIC" AND "RAPPORT" IN TONI MORRISON'S *SULA*

Barbara Johnson

Toni Morrison's novels have often been read as presenting something beloved, lost, and familiar to an African-American reader. Renita Weems, for instance, writes: "Toni Morrison is one of the few authors I enjoy rereading. Having lived in the North for the last six years (against my better senses), when I read Morrison's novels I am reminded of home: the South. Although her first three books take place in the Midwest and the fourth primarily in the Caribbean—places I have never seen—there is something still very familiar, very nostalgic about the people I meet on her pages. There is something about their meddling communities which reminds me of the men and women I so desperately miss back home" (95).

Houston Baker, in an essay entitled, "When Lindbergh sleeps with Bessie Smith," describes an equally strong sense of recognition when he writes about *Sula*:

Morrison "remembers" and enables us to know our PLACE and to be cool about our hair. For, in truth, it has often seemed in black male writings of a putatively asexual Western technological world as our proper PLACE, that the dominant expressive impulse has been more toward an escape from "bad hair" than from "bad air."

Originally presented as The Routledge Lecture, delivered on 9 May, 1992 at the University of Wales College of Cardiff. Previously published in *Textual Practice* 7.2 (Summer 1993): 165–172.

Morrison's linguistic cosmetology allows this very basic "badness" to be refigured as village value, as a mirroring language—a springy "lying" down if you will—in which we can find ourselves, and where especially black men may yet make a jubilant response, saying, "We are *that!*" (109–10)

Baker's essay is in part a response to a groundbreaking essay by Barbara Smith in which she writes of *Sula*: "Despite the apparent heterosexuality of the female characters, I discovered in re-reading *Sula* that it works as a lesbian novel not only because of the passionate friendship between Sula and Nel but because of Morrison's consistently critical stance toward the heterosexual institutions of male-female relationships, marriage, and the family" (165). How does *Sula*—a novel that holds up a mirror to black men, displaced Southerners, and black lesbians—manage to produce so strong a mechanism for recognition? How does Morrison manage to hold out so strong a promise of "home"?

One way, I would submit, is by presenting home as always already lost. The novel begins: "In that place, where they tore the nightshade and blackberry patches from their roots to make room for the Medallion City Golf Course, there was once a neighborhood" (3). Morrison's novel conveys so strong a sense of what she calls "rootedness" precisely by writing under the sign of uprootedness. Yet it is not simply that there was once a *there* there and now it is gone, but that there is from the beginning something profoundly uncanny about "that place." Home is familiar precisely to the extent that, as Renita Weems puts it, it is somehow a place one has never been. By telling the story of a lost neighborhood called the Bottom which is situated at the top of the hills, Morrison establishes home as that which is always already its own other.

This, of course, is the discovery Freud made when, in his essay on "The Uncanny," he investigated the German word for "homey." Freud exclaims over the fact that the German word for "homey" extends itself to turn into its opposite—that the meaning of "heimlich" moves with a kind of inevitability from cozy, comfortable, and familiar to hidden, secret, and strange, so that one meaning of "heimlich" is identical to its opposite, "unheimlich" (244). What Toni Morrison demonstrates in *Sula*, I think, is that that is exactly what home *is*. Morrison's perceptions about human intimacy, ambivalence, and desire intersect often with psychoanalytic paradigms and figures, but at the same time she dramatizes political and social forces that provide a larger context for what Freud generally analyzes in individuals as purely intra-psychic.

In this essay, I will look at some of the intersections between *Sula* and Freud's essay on "The Uncanny," but first, let me offer a quick sketch of the novel. *Sula* is divided into two parts separated by a ten-year interval, and into chapters entitled by dates: 1919, 1920, 1921, 1922, 1923, 1927//1937, 1939, 1940, 1941, 1965. It is preceded by a prologue from the point of view of the present. The first part of the novel describes the girlhood of two friends, Sula Peace and Nel Wright, up to the point at which Nel marries Jude Greene and Sula leaves town. When Sula returns ten years later, she is seen as evil incarnate by the townspeople because of her perceived disrespect for conventional constraints. They use her transgressiveness to define their own morality. Sula sleeps with Nel's husband, Jude, creating a rift between the two friends and provoking an unarticulated howl of grief which hovers within Nel until the very end of the novel when, after Sula's death, Nel realizes that all that time she had been mourning the loss of Sula, not Jude.

Now for a catalogue of figures Freud associates with the uncanny:

> Dismembered limbs, a severed head, a hand cut off at the wrist, ... feet which dance by themselves ... — all these have something peculiarly uncanny about them, especially when, as in the last instance, they prove able to move of themselves in addition. As we already know, this kind of uncanniness springs from its association with the castration complex. To many people, the idea of being buried alive while appearing to be dead is the most uncanny thing of all. And yet psychoanalysis has taught us that this terrifying phantasy is only a transformation of another phantasy which had originally nothing terrifying about it at all, but was qualified by a certain lasciviousness — the phantasy, I mean, of intra-uterine existence. (244)

In *Sula*, the echoes of this list are really quite uncanny. Sula's house is presided over by a one-legged grandmother, Eva, who has perhaps cut off her own leg to get the insurance money she needs to support her children, and yet who, later fearing that her grown son (who has returned from the war a drug addict) wants to crawl back into her womb, sets fire to him and kills him. Sula herself defies the teasing of a group of Irish boys by cutting off the tip of her own finger. Toni Morrison both displaces and deconstructs Freud's notion of the castration complex. On the one hand, the loss of bodily intactness is integral to survival, at least in the case of Eva. And the novel itself is written under the sign of "something newly missing": the body of a little boy named Chicken Little whom Sula and Nel have inadvertently drowned in the river. On the other hand, castration is recognized as a mechanism of social control. Sula ironically inverts familiar power relations when she answers Jude's lament that a black man has a hard row to hoe in this world by saying:

I don't know what all the fuss is about. I mean, everything in the world loves you. White men love you. They spend so much time worrying about your penis they forget their own. The only thing they want to do is cut off a nigger's privates. And if that ain't love and respect I don't know what is. And white women? They chase you all to every corner of the earth, feel for you under every bed. I knew a white woman wouldn't leave the house after 6 o'clock for fear one of you would snatch her. Now ain't that love? They think rape soon's they see you, and if they don't get the rape they looking for, they scream it anyway just so the search won't be in vain. Colored women worry themselves into bad health just trying to hang onto your cuffs. Even little children — white and black, boys and girls — spend all their childhood eating their hearts out 'cause they think you don't love them. And if that ain't enough, you love yourselves. Nothing in this world loves a black man more than another black man. You hear of solitary white men, but niggers? Can't stay away from one another a whole day. So. It looks to me like you the envy of the world. (103–04)

It could be said that what Morrison is doing is taking the Freudian concepts of envy, the penis, and castration, and recontextualizing them in the framework of American racial and sexual arrangements. It becomes impossible to speak about such terms in the abstract, universal sense in which Freud uses them once one realizes that the historical experience of some people is to be subjected to the literalization and institutionalization of the fantasies of others. Lynching dramatizes an unconscious fantasy of white men, but an historical and political reality for black men. Penis envy seems not to be confined to women at all, but to be a motive force in the repression of some men by other men. And one of the most revolutionary things Morrison does in *Sula* is to deconstruct the phallus as law, patriarchy, and cultural ground, while appreciating the penis for the trivial but exciting pleasures and fantasies it can provide for the female characters in the novel. Morrison reverses the Lacanian elevation of the phallus into the signifier of signifiers by restoring the penis to its status as an organ.

Home, then, in *Sula*, is where the phallus isn't. This may be one of the reasons for the pervasive uncanniness of the novel. But the uncanny image that sets the tone for the text as a whole involves not Sula but a young black soldier named Shadrack whose experience of the battlefield in 1917 is described as follows:

Shellfire was all around him, and though he knew that this was something called *it*, he could not muster up the proper feeling—the feeling that would accommodate *it*. He expected to be terrified or exhilarated—to feel *something* very strong. In fact, he felt only the bite of a nail in his boot.... He ran, bayonet fixed, deep in the great sweep of men flying across the field. Wincing at the pain in his foot, he turned his head a little to the right and saw the face of the soldier near him fly off. Before he could register shock, the rest of the soldier's head disappeared under the inverted soup bowl of his helmet. But stubbornly, taking no direction from the brain, the body of the headless soldier ran on, with energy and grace, ignoring altogether the drip and slide of brain tissue down its back. (7–8)

Severed heads, feet that run by themselves, this would seem a perfect image of Freud's uncanny. But I think Morrison deepens the meaning of those images by describing a *psychic* discontinuity that precedes the severing of the head. Shadrack already experiences a lack of fit between his feelings and *it*, a dissociation of expectations, an affective split.

The dissociation of affect and event is one of Morrison's most striking literary techniques in this novel, both in her narrative voice (in which things like infanticide are not exclaimed over) and in the emotional lives of her characters. The most important example of affective discontinuity is Nel's reaction to the discovery of Jude, her husband, naked on the floor with Sula, her best friend. She tries to howl in pain but cannot do so until seventy pages later when she realizes that she mourns the loss of Sula rather than Jude. A good deal of the novel takes place in the space between the moment when the howl is called for and the moment when it occurs. Similarly, the scene of the death of Chicken Little is broken up into delayed effects throughout the novel. While the chapter headings promise chronological linearity, the text demonstrates that lived time is anything but continuous, that things don't happen when they happen, that neither intentionality nor reaction can naturalize trauma into consecutive narrative. Shadrack, described by the wonderful oxymoron of "permanently astonished," institutes the *fort-da* game of National Suicide Day upon his return from the war as a way of ritually trying to get a jump on unpreparedness, but he can only repeat the lack of fit between affect and event.

For me, the most intriguing figuration of the dissociation between affect and event occurs at the moment when Nel discovers Sula and Jude naked on the floor together. While the novel as a whole is narrated in the third person, this particular passage shifts into the first person to coincide with Nel's point of view. The passage runs as follows:

When I opened the door they didn't even look for a minute and I thought the reason they are not looking up is because they are not doing that. So it's all right. I am just standing there.... And I did not know how to move my feet or fix my eyes or what. I just stood there seeing it and smiling, because maybe there was some explanation, something important that I did not know about that would have made it all right. I waited for Sula to look up at me any minute and say one of those lovely college words like *aesthetic* or *rapport*, which I never understood but which I loved because they sounded so comfortable and firm. (105)

Aesthetic and *rapport*? At a time like this, when Nel is seeing her best friend naked with her husband, why in the world is *this* the thought she turns to for an image of reassurance? The desire for an explanation, for some domain of sense that escapes her, is certainly understandable, but why does Toni Morrison pick these two words? The very arbitrariness of these two floating signifiers tempts me to see them as keys to the preoccupations of the novel as a whole.

The words "aesthetic" and "rapport" are referred to as "college words"—they thus come out of a scene included in the novel as other, not represented, not "home." (Of course, they are also from the "other scene" of the novel's author and of many of its readers.) The fact that Sula has been away to college while Nel has not does not, however, play much of a role in their friendship as it is re-established—at least not on the surface. Sula and Nel discuss college really only once, when Nel is trying to get Sula to talk about how she spent the ten years away from the Bottom:

"Tell me about it. The big city."
"Big is all it is. A big Medallion."
"No. I mean the life. The nightclubs, and parties . . ."
"I was in college, Nellie. No nightclubs on campus."
"Campus? That what they call it? Well. You wasn't in no college for—what—ten years now? And you didn't write to nobody." (99)

Nel's desire for Sula's story remains unsatisfied. We never observe a conversation between Sula and Nel that remotely resembles one in which the words "aesthetic" or "rapport" would have occurred. What we learn Nel learns in this conversation is that college is a place of foreign-sounding words. But so, for Nel, was her voyage to her roots: her grandmother's parting "voir" and her mother's admonition that she and her daughter did *not* speak Creole.

The words "aesthetic" and "rapport," in addition to coming from what could be called "another scene"—both college and foreign—also both contain silent letters, signaling their status as writing, that is, as themselves silent letters. Silent because not oral—and in writing, the sign of the oral has conventionally been the missing letter rather than the silent letter, although the missing letter is marked by a diacritical mark like an apostrophe which is all the more obviously a sign of writing in its completely unphonetic dimension. And both "aesthetic" and "rapport," somewhat like the word "unheimlich," span a wide stretch of meaning. "Aesthetic" moves from the domain of sense experience to the domain of artistic forms, while "rapport" names connection and trust but at the same time, archaically, mesmerism—a much more uncanny form of trust.

I think that in many ways the novel is precisely about the relations between aesthetic and rapport. If aesthetics is taken as the domain of the contemplation of forms, implying detachment and distance, and rapport is taken as the dynamics of connectedness, the two words name an opposition, or at least a set of issues, that are central in *Sula*. In one of the novel's primal scenes, Nel and Sula are described playing with Chicken Little, whom Sula is swinging around in circles until he slips from her grasp, flies into the river, and drowns. At the end of the novel, Eva, Sula's grandmother, accuses Nel of having thrown the little boy into the water. Nel protests that it was Sula, but Eva responds, "'You. Sula. What's the difference? You was there. You watched, didn't you? Me, I never would've watched.'" (168). Nel mulls this over in her head: "What did old Eva mean by *you watched*. How could she help seeing it? She was right there. But Eva didn't say *see*, she said *watched*" (170). Indeed, Nel has to acknowledge the unavowable memory of joy, of pleasure, that accompanied for her the spectacle of the boy slipping out of Sula's grasp. "It was there anyway, as it had always been, the old feeling and the old question. The good feeling she had had when Chicken's hands slipped."

Watching becomes even more of an issue when Hannah, Sula's mother, burns to death. Hannah's mother, Eva, leaps to try to save her. Thinking about this afterward, Eva muses:

She remembered something else, too, and try as she might to deny it, she knew that as she lay on the ground trying to drag herself through the sweet peas and clover to get to Hannah, she had seen Sula standing on the back porch just looking. When Eva, who was never one to hide the faults of her children, mentioned what she thought she'd seen to a few friends, they said it was natural. Sula was probably struck dumb, as anybody would be who saw her own mamma burn up. Eva said yes, but inside she disagreed and remained convinced that Sula had watched Hannah burn not because she was paralyzed but because she was interested. (78)

What Eva is accusing both Nel and Sula of here is a privileging of aesthetics over rapport. Contemplating with detachment, with no move to intervene, they *watch*. "Interest" is the name of a lack of involvement. Curiously, Kant defines the domain of the aesthetic as the domain of *disinterestedness*. What is the difference between interest and disinterest? Interest and disinterestedness are like heimlich and unheimlich—almost impossible to tell apart. Interestingly (uncannily?), it is precisely under the category of the aesthetic that Freud inserts his analysis of the uncanny. The first sentence of his essay begins, "It is only rarely that a psychoanalyst feels impelled to investigate the subject of aesthetics..." (219). It is as though what turns the home unheimlich cannot be fully understood without a passage through the aesthetic.

The question of aesthetics versus rapport is raised, in fact, by Toni Morrison's novel as a whole as well. The novel presents us with a series of horrible images, painful truths, excruciating losses. Do we just sit back and watch? What is the nature of our pleasure in contemplating trauma? What would be a response that would embody rapport rather than aesthetics? Is this what Toni Morrison is challenging us to consider? Or is she merely trying to make us less innocent in our contemplation, our analysis, our "interest"?

It seems to me that the challenge Toni Morrison presents to the relations between aesthetics and politics lies precisely in the uncomfortable ways in which she makes it clear that the domain of the aesthetic is both profoundly political and impossible to make politically correct. By choosing to aestheticize a father's rape of his daughter in *The Bluest Eye*, a mother's murder of her grown son and a daughter watching her mother burn to death in *Sula*, and the scars on a slave woman's back in *Beloved*, Morrison makes the aesthetic inextricable from trauma, taboo, and violation. It is no accident that the plantation from which the infanticidal slave woman has escaped in *Beloved* is called "Sweet Home." Sethe, the former slave, muses again and again about her memory of Sweet Home as aesthetically beautiful, and about *that fact* as a deep violation. On the one hand, the realm of forms—like National Suicide Day—is seen as a first line of defense against the abyss. Sula is said to be dangerous precisely because she is an artist without an art form. On the other hand, Morrison runs—indeed courts—the risk of transforming horror into pleasure, violence into beauty, mourning into nostalgia. In *Sula* she represents—in all its moral ambiguity—the problematic fascination of such transformations. Thus she shows that it is not a matter of choosing between politics and aesthetics but of recognizing the profoundly political nature of the inescapability of the aesthetic within personal, political, and historical life.

LANGUAGE THAT BEARS WITNESS
The Black English Oral Tradition in the Works of Toni Morrison

Yvonne Atkinson

Toni Morrison has said, "I tend not to explain things very much, but I long for a critic who will know what I mean when I say 'church' or 'community,' or when I say 'ancestor,' or 'chorus.' Because my books come out of those things and represent how they function in the [B]lack cosmology" (McKay, "Interview" 151). As this comment confirms, the oral tradition of Black English is the foundation of Morrison's work.

Language is more than a form of communication: it reveals the concepts that shape the significance and legacy beyond the word itself. Language defines a culture's style and method of looking at life and the individual's place within that culture. It is also "the margin," the demarcator of beauty, and the repository of a culture's defining boundaries: right, wrong, good, bad, and its liminal thresholds (Kristeva, "Ethics" 231; see also O. Davis). The study of language requires that the researcher acknowledge that the subjects being studied have a language and thereby a culture. For years the debate has raged about the language of slaves and their descendants. Today, the debate centers on whether the language spoken by most African Americans is "correct." Toni Morrison's fiction dismisses the issue of the correctness of the language, but focuses intensively upon the communal bonding and artistry evident in the language.

Some of our most learned and outspoken Americans have claimed that Africans brought to America as slaves had no art, because they lacked the necessary emotions needed to produce artistry. Thomas Jefferson said of the slave, "Their griefs are transient. Those numberless afflictions, which render it doubtful whether heaven has given life to us in mercy or wrath, are less felt, and sooner forgotten with them" (187–88). Jefferson went on to explain that this lack of feeling in the slave was the reason why the slave produced no art or literature: "Misery is often the parent of the most affecting touches in poetry. — Among the blacks is misery enough, God knows, but no poetry" (189).

When the Africans were brought to America as slaves they were denied the tools needed to create their traditional arts. Without access to these tools, the African slaves found another outlet to express the emotions of their souls: language. The language of the slaves became their canvas and clay. Their voices became the forms through which they practiced their arts. Jefferson, and others like him, were looking for the tangible presentations of art they associated with their own culture. They were looking in the wrong place. They needed to close their mouths and eyes, and listen to the voice of the African slave.

The language the African slave spoke is the foundation of the language spoken by most African Americans today: Black English. According to Geneva Smitherman, Black English is "an Africanized form of English reflecting Black America's linguistic-cultural African heritage and the conditions of servitude, oppression, and life in America. Black language is Euro-American speech with an Afro-American meaning, nuance, tone, and gesture" (*Talkin* 2). In African American culture, language is an aesthetic: "Many Black English vocabulary items manifest a poetically appropriate representation of rather mundane reality. Not only is the black lexicon a tool, its figurative power and rhetorical beauty complement its survival function" (70; see also Dillard).

Black English is a sophisticated and complex oral language in which voice and visual styling help to create meaning, what Kristeva describes as "beyond and within, more or less than meaning: rhythm, tone, color, and joy, within, through, and across the Word" (*Desire* 158). Explication in the oral tradition depends on communal knowledge, context, inflection, tone, and non-verbal gestures, as well as words. Claudia, in *The Bluest Eye*, describes this experience when she says, "we watch their faces, their hands, their feet, and listen for truth in timbre" (16).

Toni Morrison is aware of and concerned with "the language black people spoke"; as she has famously stated, the language "must not sweat. It must suggest and be provocative at the same time. It is the thing that black folks love so much — the saying of words, holding them on the tongue, experimenting with them. . . . Its function is like a preacher's: to make you stand up out of your seat, make you lose yourself and hear yourself. The worst of all possible things that could happen, would be to lose that language" (LeClair 123). The language of Morrison's texts mirrors the oral tradition of Black English. The story being told is defined by the systems of language that are evident in the oral tradition. Fitting the intricate oral tradition of language into a written form is problematic. Written language does not contain symbols to represent the inflection, tone, and non-verbal gestures of Black English. As Smitherman notes, "the real distinctiveness — the beauty — in the black sound system lies in those features which do not so readily lend themselves to concrete documentation — its speech rhythms, voice inflections, and tonal patterns" (*Talkin* 17).

As one example, in *The Bluest Eye* Morrison captures the inflection, tone, and non-verbal gestures of the oral tradition when the women's "conversation is like a wicked dance: sound meets sound, curtsies, shimmies, and retires":

> "I kind of thought Henry would marry her one of these days."
> "That old woman?"
> "Well, Henry ain't no chicken."
> "No, but he ain't no buzzard, either."
> "He ever been married to anybody?"
> "No."
> "How come? Somebody cut it off?"
> "He's just picky."
> "He ain't picky. You see anything around here you'd marry?"
> "Well. . . no." (16)

The playfulness, laughter, and camaraderie come through the written word and so do the smiles, the head-tilted-to-the-side, the "huh," and the hand-on-the-hip presence of the women. Morrison does not identify the speakers, but each line is indented, indicating a turn-taking process. The shortness of the turns implies a rapid fire, compressed conversation that is spontaneous, possibly overlapping, just like an oral conversation between friends. The reader is not told where the conversation is taking place — at a card table, in the kitchen, or over a backyard fence. Morrison leaves spaces for the reader to fill. She knows that there will be "holes and spaces" in the text that are caused by writing down an oral language, but Morrison also expects the reader to fill in those gaps with communal knowledge: "My writing expects, demands

participatory reading. . . . We (you, the reader, and I, the author) come together to make this book, to feel this experience" (Tate 164). This participatory involvement mirrors the ritual of storytelling from the Black English
oral tradition. The reader who is aware of the Black English oral tradition is
also aware that he/she is obligated to participate in this conversation. The
participation could be a "humh" at the end of the dialogue signifying understanding and appreciation, or it could be a smile, a laugh, a head wag, or it
could put you in the mind of other women who shared their lives through
conversation with friends.

The gaps and spaces created when an oral language is written down also
mirror the oral tradition's use of language as an identifying marker, a marker
of those who are part of the community and those who are not. In the African
American culture correct Black English usage demonstrates group identification. In *The Bluest Eye*, the patterns of grammar, pronunciation, vocabulary,
and language rituals that the three whores use follow the customs of Black
English oral traditions. Because they observe appropriate language characteristic of their culture, the three whores are "correct." The stark contrast
between the discourse of the whores and the description of the whores by
the narrator further illustrates their inclusion within their community. The
elevated Common English used by the narrator in the description of the
whores acts as a mirror reflecting the differences between the whores' language
and that of the narrator. This language difference duplicates code-switching
used in the Black English oral tradition. Code-switching refers to the alternating use of two different languages in a discourse. Morrison's use of code-
switching is another indication of inclusion and exclusion. The whores are
part of their community and so is the reader who understands their inclusion
without the explanation provided by the narrator.

The narrator, using elevated Common English, re-defines and re-explains
the whores in terms that can be understood by the non-Black English speaker:
"Three merry gargoyles. Three merry harridans" (47).[1] The word choice in
this description is interesting. The juxtaposition of *merry*, which suggests high-
spirited gaiety, with *gargoyle* and *harridans* illustrates the complex positions
the three whores play in the make-up of their community. (It is interesting
to note that these gargoyles, literally and figuratively, live above the Breed-
loves, just as architectural gargoyles are usually found on the top of structures.) The description of these three women as *gargoyles* and *harridans* is appropriate. They scold and can be vicious, but at the same time they are part

of a system that gives their community a form of protection. Like the gargoyles of Gothic architecture, they are the conductors of and safeguards for their community. And just in case the reader is still trying to fit these three women into the stereotypical mold of the pathetic, coarse, "prostitutes created in novels" (47), the narrator simply and totally debunks the notion. The three whores are striking and they are associated with beauty: "Poland singing— her voice sweet and hard, like new strawberries" (43). They are associated with the Black English oral tradition and are controllers and extollers of the power of the spoken word. The whores' conversation is very aural. They are storytellers who Signify, that is, they engage in the art of verbal battle, what Clarence Major defines as "'performance' talk" (416); the whores, through their Signifyin talk, pass on the beliefs and values of their community.

In Signifyin there is almost always a berating, censuring aspect to the discourse. According to Smitherman, Signifyin is "the verbal art of ritualized insult, in which the speaker puts down, needles, talks about (*signifies on*) someone, to make a point or sometimes just for fun. It exploits the unexpected, using quick verbal surprises and humor" (*Black Talk* 206). This sense of Signifyin is somewhat distinct from the way Henry Louis Gates, Jr., in his influential study *The Signifying Monkey*, understands the term. Gates's version of "Signifyin(g)" is based on "refiguring what we might think of as key canonical topi and tropes received from the black [English oral] tradition itself" (xxii). But Gates's theory does not take the "put down" aspect of Signifyin into consideration, and his theory also does not accommodate the reaffirmation of communal identity that is evident in Signifyin from the Black English oral tradition. Rather, Gates's theory is more closely related to rhetoric of the Black English oral tradition of Call/Response and Witness/Testify. While African American writers certainly "read each other, and seem intent on refiguring what we might think of as key canonical topi and tropes received from the black [English oral] tradition itself," the writers are Called on to Respond to what they have Witnessed in the works of other African American authors. Their Response becomes their Testimony and a reaffirmation of community. Gates claims to have "at last located within the African and Afro-American traditions a system of rhetoric and interpretation that could be drawn upon both as *figures* for a genuinely 'black' criticism and as *frames* through which I could interpret, or 'read,' theories of literary criticism" (ix), but he fails to ground his system of rhetoric in African American traditions; rather, the African American traditions become marginalized in his quest to "read" literary criticism (here read Eurorpean literary criticism). He says he is "attempt[ing] to lift the discourse of Signifyin(g) from the vernacular to the discourse of literary criticism" (xi), but he fails to realize that the discourse of Signifyin does not need to be "lifted" from the vernacular; rather it needs to be examined as a discourse and as a language system within the vernacular. Smitherman's definition of Signifyin, in contrast, comes from and is inclusive of traditional African American culture. She does not feel the need to legitimize Signifyin by lifting it to the heights of "Derrida's neologism" (*Signifying Monkey* 46), but rather treats the Black English oral tradition with the grace and dignity it deserves as the language system of proud people.

Signifyin is an act of delineation; it is didactic and inclusive. In the Black English oral tradition, when one is Signified on one must acknowledge the Signification. An indication of Pecola's otherness is the inversion of the Signifyin act that takes place with Pecola and the three whores. Though the three whores Signify in the presence of Pecola, they cannot be the doorway through which Pecola gains entry into the community because Signifyin in the oral tradition is age specific. The only time an adult and child participate in the act of Signifyin is in a parent/child dynamic, when the child is being taught a lesson or is being guided by the adult. Claudia and Frieda know the rules of discourse of their community: "We didn't initiate talk with grownups; we answered their questions" (22). With the whores, Pecola inverts the community rules of discourse because she initiates the conversation: "The women were friendly, but slow to begin talk. Pecola always took the initiative with Marie, who, once inspired, was difficult to stop" (44). Pecola does not participate verbally or non-verbally, staying outside of the Signifyin act:

> "All I know is, them bandy little legs of yours is every bit as old as mine."
> "Don't worry 'bout my bandy legs. That's the first thing they push aside."
> All three of the women laughed. (45)

In fact, Pecola is so far outside this communal activity that she is almost invisible or under erasure. The whores do not acknowledge Pecola's presence and talk over and around her, which, in the Black English oral tradition, signifies her "otherness." Pecola could gain entrance to her community by practicing the communal rules of discourse, but she has not learned these rules at home and so she is lost. Claudia and Frieda do not, as they should, invite Pecola into the community through their discourse with her. Like Milkman in *Song of Solomon*, Pecola needs a Pilate to guide her through this initiation, just as Pilate guides Milkman when she begins his lessons of discourse by correcting Guitar when he says, "Hi" (*Song* 36). This illustrates Morrison's concern with the act of rituals. Part of the reason that Pecola's story is told is because a necessary ritual was not performed, and thus a gap was created that needs to be closed. Thus *The Bluest Eye* can be read as a cautionary tale because, like *Beloved*, it is a story that should not be repeated.

Other examples of Black English oral traditions are the Signifyin acts of the "Three quarts of milk" soliloquy of Mrs. MacTeer in *The Bluest Eye* (22), "When Lindbergh sleeps with Bessie Smith" (145) of *Sula*, and the first private conversation between Son, "the nigger in the wood pile," and Jadine in *Tar Baby* (83, 112–27). In "Three quarts of milk" (98), Mrs. MacTeer is not only venting her anger, she is teaching her daughters one of the rhetorical tropes of their culture, how to Signify, and she is teaching them life lessons about greed and self reliance ("My mother knew that Frieda and I hated milk and assumed Pecola drank it out of greediness"); family and community values ("There's a limit to everything"); and parenting responsibilities ("'Folks just dump they children off on you and go on 'bout they business'") (22–23). Mrs. MacTeer as a caretaker of her cultural mores is an apt instructor for her children and the reader. It is important to examine what is being said as well as who is saying it.

Sula's Signifyin "When Lindbergh sleeps with Bessie Smith" speech to Nel is not only Signifyin on Nel, it is also Signifyin on America. The form of this Signification begins with a dialectic of the improbable: "'Oh, they'll love all right. . . . After all the old women have lain with the teenagers . . . after all the black men fuck all the white ones . . . when Lindbergh sleeps with Bessie Smith and Norma Shearer makes it with Stepin Fetchit'" (145–46). The contradictions of "old" and "teenager" lying together escalates to "weathervane[s]" "mount[ing] . . . hogs" (146). Sula is Signifyin on Nel and the people of the Bottom as well as on American puritanical views of sex and racial prejudices.

In *Tar Baby*, when Son Signifies on Jadine he is not only putting her down, he is also demonstrating that he is part of the community while she is not. This face-to-face confrontation takes place just after Jadine has received her coat made of "the skin of the baby seals" (112). When Jadine asks Son what his name is, he replies, "'What do you like? Billy? Paul? What about Rastus?'" (115). Rastus—the name of the Black figure on the Cream of Wheat box—is one of those names, like Sambo or Steppinfetchit, whose history brings to mind the stereotypical Uncle Tom: sleepy-eyed, lazy-acting, stupid, and buffoonish. By using this name, Son is Signifyin on Jadine. Son's use of the name Rastus also illustrates the importance of his name: "the name most truly his wasn't on any of the Social Security card, union dues cards, discharge papers. . . . Son. It was the name that called forth the true him. The him that he never lied to, the one he tucked in at night and the one he did not want to die. The other selves were like the words he spoke—fabrications of the moment, misinformation required to protect Son from harm and to secure that one reality at least" (139). The importance of his name is also a form of Signification; as Barbara Hill Rigney argues, "The primary significance of the name Son is . . . not to denote an individual self ('He did not always know who he was, but he always knew what he was like'[165]), but to place that self in a context of relationship: Son is a son of Africa and also a son of the American black male experience, the 'Nigger Jims . . . Staggerlees and John Henrys' (166) . . . his name being his . . . connection with community and black tradition" (43). Just as she earlier failed to recognize Gideon's true name, instead referring to him as "Yardman" (a serious insult in Black English, to *call out his name* and indicate disdain for his social position and his very self) (115), Jadine does not recognize the significance of Son's Signifyin or that Son's name connects him to his community. Jadine's response to Son's "Rastus" is " 'Don't be funny. What *is* your name' " (115)—which is inappropriate. She should have come back with a statement that indicated that she heard and understood his reprimand. Son is signaling to the reader that he knows who he is and what Jadine is: fragmented and outside of her community.

Morrison uses language to define those who are a part of their community and those who are not. In *Song of Solomon* Macon Dead demonstrates he is outside of his community when he breaks the language codes of the community. Macon is a landlord and Mrs. Bains is one of his tenants who has taken on the care of her grandchildren. When she comes to ask him if he will extend her some credit for her rent, he crosses the boundaries of community principles: "When Macon Dead got to the front door of his office he saw a stout woman . . . standing a few feet away. Macon unlocked his door, walked over to his desk, and settled himself behind it. As he was thumbing through his accounts books the stout woman entered" (21). Macon's actions of sitting while this elderly woman stands is just the beginning of his breach of community boundaries:

"Afternoon Mr. Dead, sir. I'm Mrs. Bains. Live over at number three on Fifteenth Street."

"Yes, Mrs. Bains. You got something for me?"

"Well, that's what I come to talk to you about. You know Cency left all them babies with me. And my relief check ain't no more'n it take to keep a well-grown yard dog alive—half alive, I should say."

"Your rent is four dollars a month, Mrs. Bains. You two months behind already."

"I do know that, Mr Dead, sir, but babies can't make it with nothing to put in they stomach."

Their voices were low, polite, without any hint of conflict.

"Can they make it in the street, Mrs. Bains? That's where they gonna be if you don't figure out some way to get me my money."

"No sir. They can't make it in the street. We need both, I reckon. Same as yours does." (21)

Macon separates himself from his community when he allows Mrs. Bains to make the first greeting, and his separation is further indicated when he later does not realize that Mrs. Bains has Signified on him. Macon does not respond; he does not participate in the Signifyin act which demonstrates his isolation. Mrs. Bains repeatedly refers to Macon as "sir," effectively putting him in the position as controller, master, or The Man, not a favorable position in the African American community (see Major 470).

In these early glimpses of Pilate and Macon the reader is shown who has the knowledge of communal mores, who is a reliable storyteller, and—crucially—who has the power of the word, *nommo*, the African concept that constitutes "the driving power... that gives life and efficacy to all things" (Jahn 101). Pilate's power and position in the community is tied to her *nommo*. She is initiator of ritual and the keeper of community. She is a griot, the figure who, as D'Jimo Kouyate describes it, "maintain[s] a cultural and historical past with that of the present.... the oral historian and educator in any given society" (Gross and Barnes 179); Pilate teaches people to know themselves and their place within their community. The first time she talks with Milkman and Guitar, she teaches them how to speak their language, and she teaches them how to listen:

"Hi."

The woman looked up. First at Guitar and then at Milkman.

"What kind of word is that?" Her voice was light but gravel-sprinkled. Milkman kept on staring at her finger, manipulating the orange. Guitar grinned and shrugged. "It means hello."

"Then say what you mean."

"Okay. Hello."

"That's better. What you want?"

"Nothin. We just passin by."

"Look like you standin by."

"If you don't want us here, Miss Pilate, we'll go." Guitar spoke softly.

"I ain't the one with the wants. You the one wants something."

"We wanna ask you something." Guitar stopped feigning indifference. She was too direct, and to keep up with her he had to pay careful attention to his language. (36–37)

Pilate not only gives these young boys a language lesson, she also demonstrates to the reader that they need to learn to "listen" carefully too. When she says, " 'You the one wants something' " to Guitar, she is alerting the reader and Guitar to an aspect of Guitar's nature that later proves prophetic.

Some of Morrison's most memorable characters wield the power of the word. They are tellers of tales: Claudia in *The Bluest Eye*, Eva in *Sula*, Pilate in *Song of Solomon*, Therese in *Tar Baby*, Baby Suggs and Sethe in *Beloved*, and the narrator of *Jazz*. These characters may not appear to be the "traditional" models of correctness and beauty, but in Morrison's novels beauty is perceived through a different lens, the lens of language. These non-traditional characters become the griots of Morrison's fictional worlds, caretakers of knowledge, guardians of history.

In Morrison's novels, as in the oral tradition, who is telling the tale is as important as the story being told. In *Song of Solomon*, both Macon and Pilate tell stories, but while Pilate is a storyteller of power, Macon lacks perception and feelings. He is isolated and fragmented, and he does not even know it, while Pilate is centered within her community. When the reader is introduced to Pilate, she has "[h]er head cocked to one side, her eyes fixed on Mr. Robert Smith, she sang in a powerful contralto: O Sugarman done fly away" (6). Her song is a story that connects to the epigraph ("The fathers may soar / And the children may know their names"), to Mr. Smith's flight, and to the stories of The Africans who Could Fly. Her song binds her to her community. Macon has lost the ability to participate in his community's oral tradition: "when he was just starting out in the business of buying houses, he would lounge around the barbershop and swap stories with the men there. But for years he hadn't had that kind of time, or interest" (52). Macon fails to participate in one of the community rituals of individual actualization through group discourse. Macon must participate or he is outside of the circle of his community. When he does not participate he is absenting himself from a ritual practice that allows all to be heard and all to listen, a practice that reaffirms the participants' membership in their community.

Reaffirmation of community is one of the hallmarks of Black English. Systems of language within the Black English oral tradition are systems that call for the participants to reaffirm their cultural roots, community, and themselves. One of those systems is Call/Response, defined by Smitherman as "stating and counter stating; acting and reacting." It is "spontaneous verbal and nonverbal interaction between speaker and listener in which all of the speaker's statements ('calls') are punctuated by expressions ('responses') from the listener." Call/Response is collaborative improvisation that is a characterization of common content and shared experience. It is also an outward expression of group that indicates a connection, a shared history and culture. It unifies the listener and the speaker. Response also allows the Caller to know that the audience approves of what she is saying and/or how she is saying it; it is immediate validation: "The process requires that one must give if one is to receive, and receiving is actively acknowledging another" (*Talkin* 119, 104, 108). In the African American community, when people pass each other in hallways, on streets, at stop lights, et cetera, they acknowledge each other's presence through verbal and/or non verbal signals; they Call and Respond to each other. Macon does not do this: "He hailed no one and no one hailed him. There was never a sudden braking and backing up to shout or laugh with a friend" (32). Macon's failure to participate in Call and Response further demonstrates his fragmentation and isolation.[2]

In *Song of Solomon,* there are layers of Call/Response when Macon stands outside of Pilate's house listening to the women inside singing: "Macon walked on, resisting as best he could the sound of the voices that followed him" (28). Pilate, Reba, and Hagar are singing a Call/ Response song to each other, but their song is also Calling to Macon: "They were singing some melody that Pilate was leading. A phrase that the other two were taking up and building on. Her powerful contralto, Reba's piercing soprano in counterpoint, and the soft voice of the girl, Hagar...pulled him like a carpet tack under the influence of a magnet" (29). This passage is also Calling to the reader to Respond. It Calls on the reader to empathize with Macon's fragmentation. The reader becomes a Witness to his isolation, loneliness, and inability to participate.

African American writers have combined the rhetoric of Call/Response with Witness/Testify, another part of the word-of-mouth facet of the African

American community: "In the African-American grain, stories were told in unceasing collaboration between the storyteller and his audience, the black community. Call-and-response was so fundamental to the form and meaning of the tales that anyone, black or white, allowed into the circle was bound to become a participant as well as a witness" (Callahan 71). Morrison allows the reader to become part of the "circle" of storytelling and thereby Witnesses. In African American culture Witness/Testify, like Signifyin and Call/Response, uses the act of communication as a metaphor for the unity expressed in the traditional African world view. The act of Witness/Testify is tangible proof that symbolizes or serves as evidence to validate one's existence as part of the group. In the oral tradition of Black English, Witness and Testify go hand in hand: one who Witnesses has an obligation to Testify. To Witness is to affirm, attest, certify, validate, and observe. Thus Smitherman defines Testifying as a "concept referring to a ritualized form of black communication in which the speaker gives verbal witness to the efficacy, truth, and power of some experience in which all blacks have shared" (*Talkin* 58).

Witness/Testify is a shared collective memory, a cultural ritual that promotes solidarity and cohesion, creating a living archive of African American culture. Witnessing is shared experience, emotional, physical, communal, historical — it is social empathy. Testifying articulates and validates the shared experience through gesture, sign, symbol, or verbal expression. In both the oral tradition and in literature, the participants of Witness/Testifying must "bear witness" to the joys and sorrows of life, and then they must Testify, tell, pass on, share the event with others. Witness/Testify assumes shared experience by the teller and the hearer: it creates and maintains spiritual kinship. Those who Witness have a responsibility to preserve and tell the tale. In written discourse, the reader becomes both symbolic and actual participant in the storytelling event through shared experience, shared emotional response, and connection made by the communal aspect of the event.

Morrison achieves this connection in *Beloved* when Baby Suggs leads the Testimony in the meetings at the Clearing:

> After situating herself on a huge flat-sided rock, Baby Suggs bowed her head and prayed silently. The company watched her from the trees. They knew she was ready when she put her stick down. Then she shouted, "Let the children come!" and they ran from the trees toward her.
>
> "Let your mothers hear you laugh," she told them, and the woods rang. The adults looked on and could not help smiling. (87)

The "company" in the Clearing are physically mirroring the spiritual kinship of the Call/Response ritual when they respond to the Call by entering the circle in the Clearing: "'Let the grown men come,' she shouted. They stepped out one by one from among the ringing trees" (87). The ritual in the Clearing is a Testimony to "the only grace they could have" (89). The reader becomes both a Witness—we are allowed to see and hear this Testimony through the written word—and a Testifier—we are Called to Respond just as the people in the Clearing are Called to respond with "their...mouths and [they] gave her the music. Long notes held until the four-part harmony was perfect enough for their deeply loved flesh" (89). Through Call/Response and Witness/Testify, Morrison make a connection between Baby Suggs, the people in the Clearing, and the reader.

In *Jazz*, the reader is a Witness for Violet, for Joe, and for the narrator. The reader is also a Witness to the story that is being told, and through discussion of the story the reader Testifies. The narrator of *Jazz* is participating in the act of Call/Response because she is a reminder, a Call to remember, all those tellers of tales, both in fiction and in life, who have sat on front porches, on stoops, at windows, and Witnessed the world pass by. This narrator follows a tradition of fictional sentries who Witness and Tell: the watchers on the porch in Zora Neale Hurston's *Their Eyes Were Watching God* and Mrs. Hedges in Ann Petry's *The Street* are characters who piece together their world from the scraps of information they glean from the lives of people around them. The reader, like these sentries, pieces together Joe and Violet's story through the fabric of language. I am a Witness to Joe and Violet's story and now you too have become a Witness and you are now obligated to Testify.

The reader who understands the implicit values and behavioral models taken from Black English oral traditions will have an understanding of Morrison's texts that "evolves out of the culture, the world, the given quality out of which [Morrison] write[s]" (McKay, "Interview" 151). Each culture has its own systems of value and beauty that are defined by language. In *Song of Solomon* Ruth may appear, to those unaware of African American culture, to be correct and beautiful while Pilate is strange and even ugly. But when viewed through the lens of their culture, Ruth is strange and Pilate is beautiful. Pilate is first described in juxtaposition to Ruth:

The singer [Pilate], standing at the back of the crowd, was as poorly dressed as the doctor's daughter was well dressed. The latter had on a neat grey coat with the traditional pregnant-woman bow at her navel, a black cloche, and a pair of four-button ladies' galoshes. The singing woman wore a knitted navy cap pulled far down over her forehead. She had wrapped herself up in an old quilt instead of a winter coat. Her head cocked to one side, her eyes fixed on Mr. Robert Smith, she sang in a powerful contralto. (5–6)

On the surface, this description seems to demonstrate the unpleasantness of Pilate's appearance in comparison to Ruth's attractiveness, but in the Black English oral tradition, the surface meaning of words is rarely the complete meaning. Definitions of words and word usage are derived from the Black English oral tradition of linguistic reversal, using negative terms with positive meanings as well as contextual meaning, a practice of exchanging or masking one linguistic process with another language known as calquing or loan translation.

Morrison uses language to define Ruth and Pilate within the social context of their community and culture. When the descriptions of Ruth and Pilate are read with a knowledge of the Black English oral tradition, the reader understands that Pilate is being praised while Ruth is being censured. The description of Ruth's and Pilate's clothing is a telling point in this narrative. Pilate is dressed "poorly" and Ruth "well" (5). Ruth's "neat gray coat" is analogous not only with wealth and prosperity, but also with Whiteness. The "traditional pregnant-woman" outfit is customary in the White community. Even the description of Ruth's hat, "black cloche," and foot wear, "four button ladies' galoshes," distinguishes her from the African American community, while the description of Pilate immerses her in her community, especially the "old quilt instead of a winter coat" (6). The narrator says Ruth "*had on* a neat gray coat," but Pilate "*wrapped herself* up in an old quilt" (5, emphasis added). Ruth is so passive that it seems as if she had been dressed by someone else, while Pilate is dynamic—she makes an active choice to wear a quilt instead of the more conventional coat. Perhaps the most revealing indicators of the description of these two women is that Ruth is voiceless while Pilate sings in a "powerful contralto" (6). In the African American culture, oral language is prized, and Pilate is a master of oral language, while Ruth is silent. Pilate, like the three whores of *The Bluest Eye*, has and uses the power of words: they sing, they are storytellers, they have the power to name and thereby define, and they are the criterion by which others are judged.

Other examples of the Black English oral traditions that Morrison uses are the references to the music that serve as filler and background in her texts: Baby Suggs's allusions in *Beloved*: "'Lay em down, Sethe. Sword and shield. Down. Down. Both of em down. *Down by the riverside*. Sword and shield. *Don't study war no more'* " (86, emphasis added); the song Halle hears that signals the time for them to escape: " 'Hush, hush. Somebody's calling my name. Hush, hush. Somebody's calling my name. O my Lord, O my Lord, what shall I do?' " (224); and Sixo's death song (225). These songs are sacred songs, songs that are emotional and historical sites. They are a communal discourse about life. They are also part of the oral tradition of Call/Response and Witness/Testify: both Baby Suggs's and Halle's songs are Call/Response songs, requiring a lead singer and an answering chorus. They also Call on the person who is knowledgeable about the oral tradition and Church to Respond with a pause — to remember other times when those songs were sung. That pause is the act of Witness/Testify and a reaffirmation of community ties.[3] Similarly, in *Jazz* traces of music flow throughout the story. Song titles ("The Trombone Blues" [21]), lyrics ("Turn to my pillow where my sweetman used to be...how long, how long, how long" [56]), and names of performers (Slim Bate's Ebony Keys [5]) add a richness to the text and infuse the story with the sound and feel of the city of the 1920s and 30s.

Morrison does not always use punctuation to identify the lyrics or titles of songs. She sometimes slips them into the narrative like a faint hum, or a radio turned down low. And just as when you hear snatches of a song from a radio, the memory of the song and the place you heard it flash through your mind, sometimes the song stays in you mind and you carry it until you hear another song. The narrator's description of the City in *Jazz* has that quality: "Big-legged women with pink kitty tongues..." (7). You can hear the song being played, or if you have not heard it before, if, as Paul D said, you do not understand the words or you do not know them, you can still understand. Through understanding, the reader participates in the event, as in the narrator's description of Dorcas's thoughts on the delicious music in *Jazz*: "Dorcus lay on a chenille bedspread...knowing that there was no place to be where somewhere...somebody was not licking his licorice stick, tickling the ivories, beating his skins, blowing off his horn while a knowing woman sang ain't nobody going to keep me down you got the right key baby but the wrong keyhole you got to get it bring it and put it right here, or else" (60). The litany of lyrics becomes like that sound right on the edge of consciousness that tantalizes the hearer/reader to listen harder, lean toward the place where the music comes from, and pay close attention. Morrison, like Pilate, is teaching the reader how to participate in the discourse of her novel and the discourse of African Americans through the uses of the Black English oral tradition.

The wonder and the beauty of Morrison's use of music in her text is that she can move you from the mourner's bench, to a jook joint, or to an up-town club in the city.[4] Morrison entices the reader's participation by leaving the music unfocused. She does not tell the reader who is singing or playing "'Hit me but don't quit me'" (59), and so the reader can determine the mood of the music by imagining the performer: Billie Holiday, feisty, determined, hard living and hard loving; Ella Fitzgerald, wistful, smooth, and bluesey; or Ben Webster with a mournful sax, crying out in despair. The music also allows the text a sense of freedom in that the mood of the music can change; it is not static. The center-less nature of the music allows the reader to participate in the Black English oral tradition of improvisation.

The plasticity of the oral tradition is also evident in its vocabulary (see Sale). *Sula's* "I disremember" (116), *Beloved's* "rememories" (95), and the "Who misraised you?" (20) of *Jazz* are all examples of how language is molded to fit the situation and the speaker. Morrison has said, "There are certain things I cannot say without recourse to my language" (LeClair 123). She uses phrases and terms that are unique to Black English: in *The Bluest Eye*, "Big Mama" (21), which means "one's grandmother, 'big' implying 'older' rather then 'larger'" (Major 325). Because the term "Big Mama" is a Southern phrase, it is a continuation, a link, not only between generations, but also between the North and the South, past and present.

In *Sula*, Eva says Uncle Paul is "Triflin'" (68), which Smitherman describes as "a person who fails to do something that he/she is capable of doing; inadequate, lazy, having no get-up-and-go" (*Black Talk* 227). The label of triflin also implicitly shows disdain and disrespect for the person it marks. Eva also tells Hannah, "'Stepping tall, ain't you?'" (68). According to Smitherman, steppin means, "Walking, often with a decisive purpose" (*Black Talk* 215). The meaning of Eva's statement refers to moving with a definite intention, knowing where you are going and how you are going to get there. It also implies that others are observing you and you are aware of this observation. Eva's "'Stepping tall, ain't you?'" in this instance means that Hannah may believe that she is special, prosperous, has some power to know where she is going, and what she is going to do once she gets there, but underlying all of this is the ironic twist that though it may seem positive, Hannah's prosperity is based on a false assumption and that she is thinking more highly of herself than she should.

In *Song of Solomon*, Guitar asks Milkman, "'What you opening your nose for?'" (102) which means, to have a strong emotional response, "to be under another's spell" (Major 325). (This phrase also has strong sexual connotations, and often describes some male or female so caught up in their sexual partner that they have lost themselves — they have given away their power to someone who could use it to destroy them.) It also implicitly means that Milkman is vulnerable because the full statement from Black English is usually something like, "Got your nose open so wide somebody could drive a truck through it." When one is "under another's spell," one is unprotected and out of control, at the mercy of someone else. Ironically, in the end it is Guitar who has his nose open, for he falls under the spell of mythical gold and Milkman is in control when he leaps into "the killing arms of his brother" (337). In *Beloved* the narrator says of Sixo's death song that it was "hatred so loose it was juba" (227). In America, Juba became the name of a dance and the term for a wild, free, joyous occasion. The juxtaposition of *hatred* and *juba* creates such a dichotomy that it establishes a dynamic image of hatred so unbounded that it is a joyous happening, rancor unleashed.

Morrison does not define or explain these terms from the Black English oral tradition in her text — indeed Morrison is frustrated at the tradition of "explanation" in African-American literature: "there was so much explanation," she says of the Black writing that preceded her, "the Black writers always explained something to somebody else. And I didn't want to explain anything to anybody else!" (Bakerman 38). For Morrison, explanation is part of the critical, not the creative, process. Morrison's use of the oral tradition helps to establish a context which in turn creates meaning in her stories. The Black English oral traditions evident in her texts evoke echoes of emotions which in turn resound between the text and the reader. Morrison has enveloped the written word in the oral tradition: the use of words from Black English and the rituals and style of the oral tradition enhance her texts, and the systems of language, the style, and the lexicon of Black English that Morrison uses in her novels bear Witness to African American culture. Following in the discourse of that culture, readers of Morrison's texts are given the opportunity — the invitation — to participate in the storytelling event.

To borrow Helene Cixious's phrase, Morrison writes with "the flesh of language" (52) from the vantage point of a people who live, and thrive, within the context of historical and political realities not of their making. The language of her texts "makes you stand up out of your seat, makes you loses yourself and hear yourself" (LeClair 123), because it is grounded in African-American culture.

NOTES

1. The traditional name given to the "correct or proper" language used by the dominant culture of the United States is usually Standard English. The word Standard sets up a hierarchy. If there is a standard than anything else must be sub-standard. The word common can also be problematic, but in this instance it refers to the discourse of the dominant community as a whole: the familiar, the prevalent method of discourse that has been designated as the language of the dominate culture.

2. In a similar instance, Morrison uses the ritual of "speaking" to define the moment in *Beloved* when Denver becomes whole and a member of her community. Stamp Paid is talking to Paul D about Denver, and states:

> "I'm proud of her. She is turning out fine. Fine."
> It was true. Paul D saw her the next morning when he was on his way to work and she was leaving hers. Thinner, steady in the eyes, she looked more like Halle than ever.
> *She was the first to smile.* "Good morning, Mr. D."
> "Well, it is now." Her smile, no longer the sneer he remembered, has welcome in it. (266, emphasis mine)

In the Black English oral tradition, the younger person acknowledges an older person. If the younger person must be prompted to do this then that person is demonstrating her/his lack of upbringing. Similarly, Morrison uses "speaking" in *Tar Baby* to demonstrate that Jadine is not part of her community because she does not participate in language rituals that are valid in the African American community: Son greets her three times with "Morning" (96) and she does not respond.

3. A particularly poignant moment of the failure of Call/Response occurs in *Beloved*, when Sixo's song Calls on Paul D but Paul D does not respond: "He thinks he should have sung along. Loud, something loud and rolling to go with Sixo's tune, but the words put him off—he didn't understand the words. Although it shouldn't have mattered because he understood the sound" (227). Sixo's death is a remembrance of an unfulfilled cultural ritual that haunts Paul D—he did not answer Sixo's Call.

4. The "mourner's bench" is usually the front pew in a traditional African American Baptist or Methodist church. During Revival, sinners, backsliders, and the unsaved sit on the mourner's bench while the saved try to convert them and bring them back into the fold. The word "jook," derived from West African languages, means wicked. In America, jook joints were, and are, places where people go to have a good time, singing, dancing, talking. They are usually little hole-in-the-wall places on the outskirts of "civilization." "Uptown club" is a term that refers to a place where the musicians feel at home. Fats Waller's song "Lounging at the Waldorf" is a signifyin song that distinguishes between uptown and downtown clubs: "Downtown we got drums but we muffle them. They [White people] like jazz, but in small doses...Uptown jazz ain't stiff with propriety." African American musicians would play downtown clubs for mostly White audiences for money, and when their set was over they would go uptown and play for mostly Black audiences.

TOWARD THE LIMITS OF MYSTERY
The Grotesque in Toni Morrison's *Beloved*
Susan Corey

Since its publication in 1987, Toni Morrison's *Beloved* has challenged and engaged readers with its moving portrayal of Sethe, an ex-slave woman, in her struggle to construct a new identity out of the horrors of her past life. Multiple plot lines, shifting points of view, and complicated chronology all contribute to the haunting effect of this novel. A crucial source of its complexity and power lies in Morrison's use of the grotesque, a multi-faceted aesthetic phenomenon that enables the artist to disrupt the familiar world of reality in order to introduce a different, more mysterious reality. This aesthetic form is well suited to carry out Morrison's desire that her work create discomfort and unease in order to confront her readers with an unfamiliar reality. She has stated that she wishes "to subvert [the reader's] traditional comfort so that he may experience an unorthodox one," whether that be "the company of his own solitary imagination" or "a reality unlike that received reality of the west" ("Memory" 387–88).

In *Beloved*, one such unfamiliar reality is the interior life of Sethe, whose subjective identity has been officially discredited and denied by the dominant culture. As female and slave, she has experienced the power of whites to harm not only the physical body, but the innermost soul: she has understood that they had the power "not just [to] work, kill, or maim you, but dirty you. Dirty you so bad you couldn't like yourself any more" (251). *Beloved* gives form to such experiences of slavery that have also left indelible effects on

America, a nation that continues to suffer the social and psychological consequences of this history of slavery and racism. On one level the novel explores the inner life of Sethe as she undergoes the difficult process of reformulating her identity, a process that requires her to confront not only the violence done to her, but also her own violent murder of her child. On another level, *Beloved* confronts readers with the shocking "otherness" of the slave experience, with their complicity in this tragedy, and with the consequences of attempting to set aside or forget this aspect of our national history.

The grotesque is well suited for this kind of exploration. Anti-rational by nature, the grotesque works to pierce conventional versions of reality, to undermine the status quo and everyday, agreed-upon assumptions, and to explore what we do not understand. While it is easier to describe than to define, I propose the following, drawn from Robert Doty, Geoffrey Harpham, and Mikhail Bakhtin, as a working definition: the grotesque is an aesthetic form that works through exaggeration, distortion, contradiction, disorder, and shock to disrupt a sense of normalcy and stimulate the discovery of new meaning and new connections. In its capacity to shock and offend, the grotesque exposes the depths of human vulnerability and the capacity for evil; in its capacity to evoke the realm of myth and mystery, it taps the resources of the body and the unconscious to open up new worlds of meaning and to expose the gaps in our conventional meaning systems (Doty, *Human Concern* 4; Harpham 51; Bakhtin 48). In *Beloved*, the grotesque aids Morrison in representing the complex social world of slavery and exposing the moral failure of the society which sustained and defended that institution. At the same time it opens doors for change and renewal to those who suffer the effects of slavery. Compatible with Morrison's high artistic standards, the grotesque achieves its effects through aesthetic means: visual imagery, paradox, distortion or degradation, and the clash of seemingly incompatible elements, all of which evoke a reader's heightened sense of awareness while avoiding sentimentality or moral harangue (Doty 4).

The term "grotesque" is derived from the Italian *grottesco* (caves), referring to a style of decorative wall painting discovered in late fifteenth century Roman excavations. An art that combined the forms of humans, animals, birds or plants in the fantastic manner of this style became known as *la grotessca* or *grottesche* (Harpham 25–26; see also Barasch and Gysin). As a phenomenon, however, the grotesque probably dates back to prehistory and the human fascination with horror and the monstrous, a fascination involving not only terror and fear, but a certain element of play or whimsy (McElroy 1, 182). Over a century ago, John Ruskin observed that "the mind under certain phases of excitement, *plays* with *terror*" (quoted in McElroy 1). This mingling of two elements—terror and play—captures what many view as the essence of the grotesque.

Two of the most original scholars of the grotesque in the twentieth century, Wolfgang Kayser and Mikhail Bakhtin, have emphasized opposing qualities of the grotesque, corresponding closely to the two elements mentioned above. Kayser focuses on fear and terror, sometimes termed the "negative" grotesque (185, 188), while Bakhtin emphasizes the elements of play, humor, and renewal, sometimes called the "positive" grotesque. In Kayser's model, the grotesque expresses primarily the alienation, estrangement, and terrifying disorder underlying daily life in the twentieth century. In contrast, Bakhtin looks back to the late medieval period where he finds the grotesque functioning as an agent of change and transformation, a reminder of a regenerating reality behind the surface of everyday life (48, 51–52). These two modes of the grotesque have also been termed the "uncanny," referring to the interior condition, and the "comic," referring to the exterior social sphere (Russo 7–8).

Bakhtin claims that the positive version of the grotesque, found in early Renaissance Europe, particularly in the work of Rabelais, has been absent in literature for well over a century, corresponding to the loss of folk culture (109). Indeed, the "negative" grotesque has been very prominent in the work of twentieth century artists. I would argue, however, that Toni Morrison has discovered new possibilities for the grotesque by employing both modes, the negative, or "uncanny," grotesque and the positive, or "comic," grotesque in her fiction, thus using the grotesque to its fullest capacity as a meaning-making tool. In this respect, she follows in the tradition of another master of the grotesque, Flannery O'Connor (Gentry 12).

In *Beloved*, Morrison establishes a dialectic between these two poles of the grotesque to maintain a tension between the interior and exterior experiences of slavery and between the historical past and the realm of the uncanny. The grotesque not only reveals the horror of slavery, but it also sets forth a vision of regeneration and healing. Morrison uses the grotesque in its negative mode to explore the destructive nature of the slave system, exposing its damage to lives and communities over generations. In its positive mode, the grotesque suggests the possibility of recovery as the characters become connected to the resources of their bodies, their emotions, and their ancestral traditions.

Through this aspect of the grotesque, Sethe and Paul D begin the process of recovering and integrating lost memories and repressed parts of themselves, a prerequisite to being able to envision a future.

Examples of the negative grotesque begin on the first page of the novel with the haunting of Sethe's home by the "baby ghost," evidence of the eruption of disorder amid the daily lives of Sethe and her family. The strange voices, lights, and violent shaking caused by this ghost have seriously disrupted the normalcy of Sethe's family life, frightening her and her daughter, Denver, and causing her sons to leave home. These opening scenes alert the reader that this story involves that border region between the mundane world and the realm of mystery or the uncanny. For Sethe the ghostly signs are concrete reminders of her guilt for the murder of her baby some eighteen years ago. The physical shaking urges her to break out of her normal routine and to confront directly this ghost of guilt from her past.

One of the most powerful grotesque images in the novel is the deforming, tree-shaped scar which Sethe bears on her back and reveals to the former slave, Paul D, soon after his arrival at 124. It is a clear example of the qualities of physical deformity, degradation, paradox, and ambiguity typically associated with the grotesque. Its decorative, viney quality recalls the style of grotesque painting discovered in the ancient Roman *grotte,* and like many grotesque images its effect is both repulsive and attractive, signifying the complexity of Sethe's relationship to her past. As the physical inscription of a brutal humiliation and beating by the slave master, Schoolteacher, the scar recalls the horror of that historical past. In order to support his theory of racial inferiority, Schoolteacher had ordered his nephews to "take [Sethe's] milk" as part of an experiment to demonstrate the "animal" characteristics of blacks. Sethe was not only required to submit to this degradation, but also to participate by making the ink with which Schoolteacher recorded the results of his experiments. This scene shocks the reader with unspeakable horror and serves as a prime example of slavery's destructive effects on the imagination and the inner life. As Sethe reflects, the whites could "dirty you so bad you forgot who you were and couldn't think it up" (251). The deadened scar tissue on Sethe's back is emblematic of her repressed feelings related to this experience. The taking of her milk has affected her more profoundly than the physical beating that followed. As she recalls, "The picture of the men coming to nurse her was as lifeless as the nerves in her back where the skin buckled like a washboard" (6). The scar, then, becomes a bodily sign of

Sethe's estrangement from her imagination and her inner life. Like the deadened nerves that alienate her from her bodily sensations, the "lifeless" picture represents the blocked memory and emotions that separate her from a full, subjective identity. As an element of the grotesque, the scar also functions as a sign of degradation, which Bakhtin explains as the process of bringing an elevated ideal or quality down to earth, to the physical level (20–22). In this respect, the scar and its link to the "experiment" on Sethe degrades both the ideology of slavery and the "Christian" society that upheld it by exposing the brutal consequences of those theories on the interior as well as the exterior lives of its victims.

However, Morrison maintains a dialectical tension in her use of this image — it is not merely negative. In its resemblance to a tree, the scar recalls the natural beauty and the qualities of comfort and renewal that Sethe associates with her former home. Unable to see the scar herself, Sethe remembers that Amy, the white girl who delivered her baby, described it as a blossoming tree — " 'Your back got a whole tree on it. In bloom' " (79) — and she repeats Amy's words to Paul D: " 'a chokecherry tree. Trunk, branches, and even leaves' " (79). In Sethe's mind, the tree might even be bearing fruit: " 'Could have cherries too now for all I know,' " she tells Paul D (16). In this respect, the scar acts as the positive grotesque, suggesting the possibilities of renewal through the natural cyclical processes of the body, a prominent theme for Bakhtin, for whom the grotesque affirms the human connection to "the material and bodily roots of the world" (19).

Paul D also experiences the ambiguous effects of the scar. He sees it first as a wrought iron sculpture filled with unexpressed emotion, "like the decorative work of an ironsmith too passionate for display" (17). When he touches the tree-like scar with his cheek, he contacts Sethe's deep sadness: he feels "her sorrow, the roots of it; its wide trunk and intricate branches" (17). Later, however, it appears to be simply "a revolting clump of scars," nothing like a tree, since trees were "inviting; things you could trust and be near; talk to if you wanted to" (21).

These contradictory connotations of the scar suggest the ambiguity of Sethe's relationship to the landscapes of her past, a relationship reinforced by her memory of the beautiful sycamore trees of Sweet Home, treasured despite their painful association with the hangings of her fellow slaves: "Although there was not a leaf on that farm that did not make her want to scream, it rolled itself out before her in shameless beauty. . . . Boys hanging from the most beautiful sycamores in the world. It shamed her—remembering the wonderful soughing trees rather than the boys" (6). Through the imagery of trees, an experience of horror and degradation is linked to a contrasting picture of beauty, comfort, and the ongoing life of the natural world. This clash of incompatible elements is a salient feature of the grotesque, contributing to its interpretive energy by stimulating readers to discover new connections and new meaning (Harpham 187).

In its negative mode, then, the scar is an emblem of Sethe's suffering, degradation, and fear which has marked her psychically as well as physically. As such, it links her to a number of other characters who bear grotesque deformities, bodily signs of their inner suffering: Baby Suggs, who had injured her hip as a slave and walked with a limp; Sethe's mother, Ma'am, who bore the burned mark of a cross on her skin; Nan, Sethe's wet nurse, who was missing half of one arm; Ella, marked with "scars from the bell . . . thick as a rope around her waist" (258); and Paul D, who carried the mark of the iron collar on his neck, "three wands like attentive baby rattlers curving two feet into the air" (273; see Ledbetter 42–45). These physical deformities, all marks of the grotesque, serve to heighten the reader's consciousness of the monstrous character of slavery written on the bodies of its victims. In its positive or "comic" mode, however, the scar signifies the renewing processes of life: in this case, the mystery and wonder of Sethe's survival and renewed strength as she gives birth to Denver and journeys toward Baby Suggs and freedom in Ohio, a journey with mythic overtones recalling the birth of Moses and the Israelites' journey out of Egypt.

Throughout the novel, Morrison sustains a dialectical tension between these two modes of the grotesque, not allowing her fiction to rest in either one. The moments of renewal and hope tend to dissolve into scenes of fear and alienation. Even Sethe's hopeful journey has its negative side, leading ultimately to the moment of madness when she murders her baby—a grotesque event in its shocking violence, and one that renders Sethe a grotesque figure in the eyes of her community. In the various accounts of this event, Morrison employs the paradoxical features of the grotesque to present a complex vision of Sethe's community. Like Bakhtin and his model, Rabelais, she celebrates the potential of the community to provide resources for renewal and hope and to sustain traditional folk values. However, Morrison is critical of the community's failure to love and forgive. She portrays the community's failure to grasp the broader context of Sethe's act or to empathize with her conviction that death would be preferable to life under slavery. Rather than looking within, the community projects its fears onto Sethe, casting her as a grotesque figure who has transgressed all bounds of normalcy and, together with her family, must be strictly avoided. This critical perspective on the community is an example of an important quality of the grotesque in African-American literature: "the simultaneous presence of a total involvement in the black experience and its critical appraisal from an extreme emotional distance" (Gysin 89–90). The grotesque always insists on the mixed nature of human existence.

The most obviously grotesque character in the novel and the one most responsible for introducing dissonance and shock into the lives of the protagonists is Beloved. As the physical embodiment of Sethe's murdered daughter, as well as those thousands who died during the middle passage, Beloved resembles one of the African river goddesses who easily crosses boundaries between the living and the dead (see Cliff). She represents the eruption of the uncanny, the anti-rational, or the mythic into the realm of normal existence, an event that may unlock previously locked emotions and open the mind to a wider experience of life. According to traditional African cosmology, Beloved could also be a potentially dangerous spirit because of her unnatural death. Peter Paris writes that in African cosmology those who die an unnatural death cannot be ancestors; hence a spirit who suffers an unnatural death is capricious and "not easily pacified" since it has lost its family and community moorings (52–53).

Like other grotesques, Beloved is a contradictory figure — positive and negative, attractive and repulsive. Both beautiful and freakish, she is abnormally strong with expressionless eyes, capable of changing shape and character or of becoming invisible. As a positive or comic grotesque, Beloved functions in the realm of fantasy and interior space where she promotes healing and growth for Sethe and Paul D, both of whom have closed off their emotional lives following their traumatic past experiences. Their contact with Beloved raises questions they have avoided and sets in motion the recovery of repressed memories, a connection that is painful but crucial for the process of rebuilding self identity. Beloved's questions direct Sethe to memories of her past, so painful that it was previously "unspeakable" (58); they lead Paul D to the "ocean-deep place he had once belonged to" (264), a level of reality beyond language. Yet Beloved also contributes to the dialectical tension between the positive and negative grotesque. She is dangerous in her exaggerated neediness, her desire to possess Sethe completely and to take her to "the other side." Her demands magnify Sethe's mother-guilt and encourage her obsessive effort to make amends for the murder to the point of nearly giving up her life, becoming death-focused and mired in the past.

Beloved first appears in fleshly form in the context of a carnival, an event closely associated with the positive grotesque. In Bakhtin's view, the medieval spirit of carnival embodies the basic impulse for the grotesque: it frees the world from fear and offers temporary liberation from the established hierarchies of class and rank (10, 19). Beloved appears immediately after Paul D, Sethe, and her daughter Denver return from such a carnival. Performed for an all-black audience on "Colored Thursday," the carnival has temporarily upset the social order. The audience has laughed at the grotesque characters, temporarily dethroning the ideal of white supremacy: "seeing white people loose: doing magic, clowning, without heads or with two heads, twenty feet tall or two feet tall" (47–48). Despite having to endure a few insults themselves, the black community has enjoyed laughing at "the spectacle of white folks making a spectacle of themselves" (48). In Bakhtin's model, laughter is a means of overcoming fear and celebrating a common humanity (11, 47). In the same way, the carnival laughter has allowed the black community to erase temporarily any fear of white folks' "otherness" and to view them from a new perspective. It has even altered some intra-community attitudes: Denver notices that after eighteen years of shunning, some women have dared to smile at Sethe (48). For Bakhtin, the carnival prepares the way for change by freeing the imagination to play with an alternative world view (49). In this sense it is a fitting prelude to the arrival of Beloved, who disrupts the lives of Sethe and her family and opens them to the possibility of change and renewal.

Images of the open body are further signs of Beloved's affinity with the positive grotesque. Immediately after Beloved arrives, Sethe experiences strong, physical symptoms of release — an uncontrollable urge to urinate, followed by a rush of water so strange and overwhelming that she feels like a carnival freak. Beloved herself consumes large quantities of water, followed by episodes of incontinence during her four days of deep sleep (51, 54). These images of bodily release are examples of what Bakhtin calls the grotesque body — the open body of becoming that affirms connections with the material and bodily roots of the world. In his analysis, images of eating and drinking or of open bodily orifices suggest openness to the world and the ongoing processes of life (26–27, 281). Yet Beloved has an equal affinity with the negative grotesque or the uncanny. She is a fascinating playmate for Denver until, in a game of hide-and-seek, Denver is terrified by Beloved's ability to magically appear and disappear (123). For Sethe and Paul D, Beloved serves as a catalyst to awaken their emotions and memories, but she also arouses their fears. Her dual aspects are continually apparent.

Paul D discerns an uncanny quality about Beloved from the outset as she sets out to take his place beside Sethe. Soon after her arrival, he finds himself being mysteriously moved out of Sethe's house, even as he had earlier evicted the "baby ghost." In the darkness of the cold house, where he has come to spend his nights, Beloved mysteriously appears and subjects him to a grotesque seduction, insisting that he touch her "inside part" and call her name (117). He resists her overtures, just as he resists confronting the painful memories of his last days at Sweet Home — the sight of his closest companions hung, sold, or reduced to idiocy, and the brutalizing experiences on the chain gang. Feeling ashamed and guilty over these encounters with Beloved, Paul D experiences physical signs of her uncanny effect — "a shudder" and "a bone cold spasm" (235) — when Stamp Paid mentions her name.

Nevertheless, these sexual encounters are important for Paul D's recovery of self. The arousal of his bodily responses is accompanied by an awakening of his emotion and memories: the lid of the "tobacco tin" protecting his heart gives way, leaving him vulnerable to the repressed emotions from his past — his feelings of guilt at his failure to join Sixo, who had laughed in the face of fear; and his shame at being harnessed with a bit, so that even Brother, the rooster, seemed to laugh at him. Although confronting these memories is exceedingly painful, Paul D later admits his gratefulness to Beloved for escorting him toward that "ocean-deep" place (264). Through his contact with her, Paul D has begun to reconnect to his body, his emotions, and his unconscious memories.

The effect of Beloved on Sethe is more complex, although similarly ambiguous. Beloved's questions and her demand for stories stimulate Sethe's memories of her childhood and her own mother, whom she barely knew. In telling these stories, Sethe experiences an awakening of pain and anger as she recalls the mother who was not allowed time to nurse her, the mother who was hanged for some unknown offense. Yet the stories also evoke positive memories—events or images that suggest hope for renewed ties with the community or with the lost or repressed part of the self .

One of these memories is the healing power of physical touch that Sethe first experienced at the hands of Amy, the mysterious white girl who rubbed Sethe's bruised and torn feet following her escape from Sweet Home, dressed the wounds on her back, and assisted in the delivery of Denver. Another is the memory of Baby Suggs, Sethe's mother-in-law, who proclaimed the healing power of the body in her preaching and practiced it on Sethe. Both memories focus on the physical body as an important site in the process of transforming identity.

Following her liberation from slavery, Baby Suggs formed a congregation in the Clearing where she preached a religion of joy that loved and affirmed the physical body. Hers was a subversive message, an effort to counter years of social conditioning which had denied slaves the capacity to experience bodily pleasure and joy. Sethe remembers how each week Baby Suggs exhorted her congregation of ex-slaves to love the flesh: "'Love it, love it hard. . . . Love your hands! Love them. . . . Touch others with them. . . . *You* got to love it, *you!*'" (88). Convinced of the renewing power of the flesh, Baby Suggs urged the people to love even their inside parts, as a way of triumphing over the years under white masters, who despised their bodies: "'This is flesh I'm talking about here,'" she said, "'Flesh that needs to be loved'" (88). Through the ritual power of dance, song, and imagination, Baby Suggs offered her congregation the possibility of transforming their memories, exhorting them especially to love the heart, "'for [it] is the prize'" (89).

In its communal and physical nature, this scene clearly evokes the positive grotesque. Like Bakhtin, Baby Suggs has faith in the renewing power of the communal body as a means of connection, not merely to their individual bodies, but to the regenerative power of the "collective ancestral body of all people" (Bakhtin 19, 24). It is a scene of carnival spirit, encouraging the spirit of imaginative play while suspending the customary cultural norms, both important in the process of social and individual transformation.

Sethe personally experiences the power of physical touch in Baby's attention to her wounded body following her arrival at 124. This ritual experience of washing and massaging is followed by Sethe's sensual joy in her ability to nurse both babies, an experience that temporarily erases the horror of her experience with Schoolteacher's nephews. These bodily experiences together with the celebratory feast following Sethe's arrival all point toward the "positive" or comic grotesque.

Yet Morrison continues the dialectic, undercutting the positive with the negative. Baby Suggs's healing touch becomes a stranglehold, as Beloved exerts her mysterious powers. Years after Baby Suggs's death, when Sethe returns to the Clearing hoping to relive the experience of those soothing hands, a gentle neck massage suddenly becomes a terrifying chokehold, a reminder of Beloved's demonic purpose. Similarly, the earlier scene of a joyous reunion feast celebrating Sethe's liberation serves as a prelude to horror.

Morrison's description of the feast is rich with allusions to the mythic and the sacred (see Harpham 51, and O'Connor 42), particularly to holy communion and the Last Supper. It begins with just a few buckets of blackberries donated by Stamp Paid, the man who ferried Sethe and the baby to freedom; then it expands to become a banquet for ninety with turkey, new peas, and pies, made with "berries that tasted like church" (136), reminiscent of the biblical accounts of miraculous feedings. In one sense it is an event of reckless generosity, representing the joyful connections of community and the pleasures of reunion and freedom, signs of the positive grotesque. Eating and drinking are important aspects of the grotesque body, whose character is to be open and unfinished, acknowledging the on-going creative processes of life (Bakhtin, 26, 281). For Bakhtin, the banquet feast in the early modern period signifies the symbolic unity of working people and the triumph of life over death (281–83). Baby Suggs's feast, then, can be read as yet another occasion for promoting altered perspectives.

Such a celebration of communal sharing is duplicated in the biblical stories of the feeding of the five thousand and in the eucharistic meal itself. But like the Mardi Gras preceding the season of Lent, the mood of joy is diminished by the allusions to the Last Supper with its overtones of betrayal, suffering, and tragic death—of sorrow mixed with joy. The imagery of blood and wine evoked by the berries and the thorny bushes leaves no doubt about the intended connection to Christ's suffering on the way to the cross. The narrator describes how picking the berries had left Stamp Paid with bleeding hands, but "to eat them was like being in church. Just one of the berries and you felt anointed" (136). In fact, Stamp sacramentally places one of the berries in baby Denver's mouth. Yet this is no solemn ritual: the sight of Stamp's bloody hands, recalling Jesus' crown of thorns, prompts Baby Suggs to erupt in hearty laughter at his grotesque appearance: "When Baby Suggs saw his shredded clothes, bleeding hands, welted face and neck she sat down laughing out loud" (136), a sign of the reigning spirit of carnival, "the ever-laughing principle which uncrowns and renews" (Bakhtin 24).

But the gaiety is only momentary. This joyous banquet intended to bring the community together has precisely the opposite effect. The envy and disapproval aroused in the community and the world-shattering arrival of Schoolteacher suggest the transitory nature of such joyous events. While the community does not directly betray Sethe, as Judas betrayed Jesus, they betray her indirectly, like Peter, in their failure to warn her of the coming danger (157). Perhaps it was due to their envy and anger over what, to them, was Baby Suggs's hubris at hosting such an extravagant feast: "Too much, they thought. Where does she get it all.... Loaves and fishes were His powers— they did not belong to an ex-slave" (137). Stamp Paid believes it was simply "meanness" that caused the community to fail to notice the approach of "the four horsemen" (157), the apocalyptic moment for Sethe. Thus, Morrison calls attention to the collaboration of the black community in Sethe's fate, refusing to represent blacks only as victims.

The arrival of Schoolteacher and his crew, together with the community's envy and jealousy, marks an eruption of the negative grotesque—fear and disorder disrupting the communal banquet and exposing the ruthless nature of the ruling "Christian" order. Like Beloved, these are grotesque figures who have crossed over from another world, a metaphoric world of the dead, and threaten to bring Sethe and her children back with them. Not hesitating to choose the realm of the dead over the death-dealing world of slavery, which kills the self, if not the body, Sethe murders her baby.

The feast of celebration, then, embodies both aspects of the grotesque. Externally, it is an event of communal sharing and togetherness, marred by its opposite—a scene of horror and bloody child murder. Internally, it evokes a sense of the sacred and the transcendent, yet arouses anger and alienation, bringing discord and division to the community. At a later communal gathering, after the burial of Baby Suggs, the positive associations with feasting seem to have completely broken down. People refuse to eat Sethe's food, and she theirs. The potential for renewal through communal eating is present, but undermined by negative emotions. As Stamp Paid recalls, the dance at Baby's funeral was one of "pride, fear, condemnation and spite" (171). In symbolically rejecting Baby Suggs's family, the community is also rejecting the possibility of an altered relationship with the world represented by Schoolteacher.

In the midst of this rupture between the community and Sethe, Beloved appears. In the scenes following Paul D's departure from 124, Beloved employs her playful, imaginative qualities. Presenting Sethe with a pair of ice skates, Beloved initiates a period of play and laughter which becomes grotesque in its exaggerated, out-of-control effects. This is a liminal period when time seems to stop. It is marked by ambiguity, psychic and physical danger as well as physical transformation. It is the sort of occasion which lends itself to the grotesque, which often operates during periods of change or transition (Bakhtin 9).

An evening of ice skating is filled with laughter as the three women slip and slide on the pond. However, as the days pass, we are reminded of Beloved's uncanny presence. When Stamp Paid pays two abortive visits to 124, he is put off by the sounds of ghostly voices, the roaring of "the people of the broken necks," all those "black and angry dead" with their "undecipherable language" (181, 198). This is clearly a realm of the uncanny and the irrational. During these days, the game-playing of the women escalates to the point where Sethe and Beloved become completely absorbed with each other. Dressing like carnival women, they wind flowers all over the house, exchange roles of mother and daughter, and alter their physical shapes. Sethe diminishes as Beloved grows larger, not only physically, but in her psychic power. The references to carnival dresses, freakish shapes, and bodily transformation again signal the presence of the positive grotesque which promotes transformation and renewal. Indeed, this liminal period of play seems important for the creative work of Sethe's imagination as she subconsciously begins to integrate her painful memories and to formulate an answer to Beloved's questions about the murder. But it is also life-threatening, indicated by the roaring of those spirits who would lead Sethe out of the material world.

For Denver, this grotesque playtime has a positive, growth-producing effect. She has come to understand her mother's fear that Beloved might leave before she could convince her that she had killed her out of "true love" (251). Recognizing that Sethe's intense inner struggle threatens her physical survival, Denver claims her own humanity and assumes adult responsibility by moving out of this ghostly household to seek help in the community.

Sethe is returned to the material, human world through the agency of Denver and a group of community women who perform a ritual exorcism.

This scene is nearly a literal representation of Wolfgang Kayser's model of the grotesque. Kayser suggests that the grotesque functions primarily as a way to "invoke and subdue the demonic aspects of the world"; that is, it allows the artist to call upon and confront the demonic in order to cast it out (188). This seems to be exactly what is taking place toward the end of the novel. Having heard about Sethe's plight from Denver, a community of women gather in an attempt to drive out the ghost of Beloved, who is threatening Sethe's life. These are the very women who have shunned Sethe for eighteen years, but whose change of heart may be, in part, due to the presence of the grotesque in their midst, shaking up their normal ways of seeing and behaving. Word from Denver about this ghost's fleshly manifestation has so outraged the women that thirty of them are moved to cross over their self-constructed boundaries and march to Sethe's home. There they intend to face down evil and drive out the huge, naked figure of Beloved, who has assumed a goddess-like appearance, pregnant with a dazzling smile and viney hair. It is a hot day, filled with the stench of sewers, hanging meat, and small, dead animals, suggesting the hostile atmosphere of this spiritual battleground: "Trust the devil to make his presence known" (258), the narrator tells us. At the same time, the references to sewers and meat may point toward the "lower bodily stratum," the materiality of Bakhtin's positive grotesque. The women's concern offers hope that Sethe might overcome her estrangement and reestablish her ties to the community, a step in the process of reconfiguring her identity.

In contrast to earlier scenes of community, marked by hostility and envy, Morrison here invokes the positive powers of the communal body as a force against evil. As the women recall their memories of Baby Suggs, they move into a ritual that connects them to the ancient sources of their tradition and begin to pray and holler, a holler that went "back to the beginning [when] there were no words" (259). The power of their cry, a sound that recalls a primal time before words, lies in the realm of the body and its renewing powers. As she hears the voices of the women searching for "the sound that broke the back of words" (261), Sethe experiences a moment of healing and communion. Standing in the doorway, holding hands with Beloved, with the sound breaking over her, "she trembled like the baptized in its wash" (261). This is a sacred moment, like the ritual of baptism that ushers one into community and promises renewal and forgiveness. This scene, then, becomes more than merely invoking and subduing the demonic. Morrison has dissolved the negative grotesque into the positive, and the exorcism becomes a moment of deep mythic connection with the ancestral traditions of this community.

And yet the novel still continues the dialectic. In a near replay of the banquet scene before Schoolteacher's appearance, this sacred moment erupts in horror. At the very moment that Sethe experiences a connection to Baby Suggs and her healing power, she sees her white benefactor, Mr. Bodwin, enter the yard. She feels hummingbird wings in her hair—a repetition of the former experience—and runs with her ice pick to attack him (compare page 163). It is unclear just what lies behind this action. Perhaps Sethe has confused Bodwin with Schoolteacher and is reliving that experience, determined this time to kill him, rather than her child. Or perhaps she has become an instrument of Beloved's will, carrying out her desire to kill the man who saved her mother from hanging and thus from joining Beloved in death. Such ambiguity is, of course, typical of the grotesque. Regardless of Sethe's motive, it is Denver who stops her, protecting the white man, but also saving her mother from a sure hanging and averting racial violence. Like her "namesake" Amy, Denver provides a link to the white community and a sign of potential interracial healing. At the same moment, Beloved disappears. The exorcism appears to have been a success, at least temporarily, although Beloved's presence lingers in the background: "A naked woman with fish for hair" (267) has been seen by the stream behind 124.

Beloved's departure from the story does not end the presence of the grotesque, for it continues to operate in other forms and images. After Beloved disappears, Paul D returns to Sethe's house to discover the aftermath of her fantastic interlude. He finds her house transformed into a grotesque jungle: dead ivy twined around poles, and the place full of dead plants, rotting stems, shriveled blossoms, dead bugs, and flowers in a riot of color—all signs of the disorderly, anti-rational character of the grotesque. Although Sethe continues in a state of profound withdrawal after her ordeal, Paul D has apparently undergone a changed consciousness following his encounter with the grotesque. Having confronted and worked through his personal pain and guilt, he has gained a new empathy for Sethe's tragic past, and has come to draw her back to life, by proposing that the two of them—she with her "wrought-iron back" and he with his own grotesque "neck jewelry"— might put their stories next to each other and find a future together. He has come to accept her as a "friend of [his] mind" and to convince her that, indeed, she has a self worth preserving (272–73). We are not told whether Sethe will accept his offer, but we know, through Denver's account, that Sethe has faced her own violent action from the perspective of the victim, and that she has managed to articulate to Beloved (and herself) the experiences, emotions, and thoughts that led up to the murder. She has been able to construct a coherent story from her disparate feelings and memories (251). Thus, although Beloved nearly succeeded in leading Sethe to join her in death, whether literal or psychic, she has also functioned in a comic or redemptive mode, serving as a catalyst for change and renewal for both Sethe and Paul D.

In true grotesque style, however, the ending of the novel remains ambiguous, refusing to offer any final or closed version of the truth. We cannot be sure what kind of future these characters will have: Denver has acknowledged a new-found "self to look out for and preserve" (252) and has moved back into the community. Her future seems hopeful, although there is the nagging hint that the Bodwins might simply be updated versions of Schoolteacher: Denver reports that Mrs. Bodwin plans to "experiment on her" and may send her to Oberlin. Although Paul D does not voice his distrust of white schoolteachers, the ambiguity remains. Readers are also left wondering whether the community will welcome Sethe or whether she will continue to remain an outcast; whether the haunting has truly ended, or whether Beloved will return to disturb Sethe and the community. The grotesque is always ambiguous, always in process.

In fact, the final, meditative section directly undercuts the hopeful tone of the reconciliation scene to end the novel on a dissonant note. Here the narrator speaks about the loneliness of the ghost who has been forgotten by the community, "disremembered and unaccounted for" (274), but who still roams in her loneliness and occasionally brushes a cheek in sleep. No longer a fleshly presence, Beloved's earlier fears of breaking apart have been realized: she has broken up "into her separate parts" and, like Son in Morrison's *Tar Baby*, has moved back to the world of myth and dreams. The mournful tone of this section seems to convey a final word of judgment on the community for its refusal to remember this ghost from the past or to incorporate her story into their history. "It was not a story to pass on," the narrator insists; yet the story-teller has indeed passed it on, challenging the community's and the reader's desire to forget. While the grotesque can be "a trigger for blasting complacency" (Doty, *"human concern"* 5), it is probably human nature for a community to resist or fear such challenges to normalcy. People do not give in to such challenges, the narrator tells us, "because they know things will never be the same if they do" (275).

As readers, we recognize ourselves in this judgment. In fact, the narrator may be speaking not merely about Sethe's immediate community, but about America as a whole, which would prefer to let such shocking pieces of its national history fade into the past. If Sethe and Paul D need Beloved as a catalyst to recover their life stories and move into a wider realm of meaning, it may be that America also needs an encounter with the grotesque to shake the foundations of its national experience and come to terms with its violent and fragmented history. Here we recall William Faulkner, who also employed grotesque characters to confront readers with America's racism. In any case, Beloved remains in the background as a haunting presence who reminds the community of those "Sixty Million and more" untold stories of slavery and the middle passage, which Morrison cites in her epigraph.

It would be a mistake to interpret this novel solely in terms of the grotesque—that would do an injustice to its rich complexity. The point is rather to appreciate how Morrison has employed this aesthetic form in *Beloved*, using its full range of possibilities, both negative and positive, to push her fiction "outward," in Flannery O'Connor's words, "toward the limits of mystery" (41). The grotesque has aided the novelist in addressing political and moral issues without sacrificing artistic quality. With its capacity to surprise, shock, and disrupt complacency, the grotesque brings readers to a heightened state of awareness and involves them in the process of making meaning. With its strong visual qualities, the grotesque confronts us as readers in the most intimate ways. When Stamp Paid considers the tiny hair ribbon knotted to the curl of wooly hair and asks, "'What *are* these people? You tell me, Jesus. What *are* they?'" (180), we readers cannot hide our eyes, but must face the moral questions. Yet in its ability to invoke laughter and the realm of myth and the spirit, the grotesque lends the promise of hope to the novel—not a utopian hope, but one based on the potential for human beings and societies to continue to change and grow. Morrison has referred to her admiration of the African American tradition of telling tales in such a way that they linger in the readers' imaginations: "The folk tales are told in such a way that whoever is listening is in it and can shape it and figure it out. It's not over just because it stops. It lingers and it's passed on. It's passed on and somebody else can alter it later. You can even end it if you want" (Darling 253). Such is precisely the final effect of the grotesque in this novel: it provides a haunting quality that causes *Beloved* to linger in the mind, continuing to provoke new discoveries long after the book has been put away.

From the Sublime
to the Beautiful
The Aesthetic Progression of Toni Morrison

Marc C. Conner

The great truism of Morrison scholarship is that her primary theme is "community."[1] Certainly each novel rigorously engages such issues as what constitutes a community, what function a community serves, what threatens a community, what helps it survive. As Morrison herself has said, "If anything I do, in the way of writing novels (or whatever I write), isn't about the village or the community or about you, then it is not about anything" (Leonard 706). The relationship between the individual and the community is indeed the central concern of Morrison's rich narratives; yet the complexity of this relationship has in many respects gone largely unnoticed. Most readers view Morrison's emphasis on community in an overwhelmingly positive light, seeing the community as nurturing, cohesive, and healing, and the individual's place within that community as one of security and comfort.[2] But in fact the communities depicted throughout Morrison's fiction, from *The Bluest Eye* to *Paradise*, are predatory, vampiric, sterile, cowardly, threatening; and the individual must struggle desperately to survive in the midst of this damaging community—a struggle that is often a losing one, resulting in the fragmentation and destruction of these desperate selves.

Morrison's engagement with the relations between the individual and the community reveals a striking progression. In her early novels, *The Bluest Eye* and *Sula*, the individual and the community are clearly opposed to one another, and the community ruthlessly victimizes the individual, ultimately de-stroying both Pecola and Sula. The two novels that follow, *Song of Solomon* and *Tar Baby*, work to reconcile the self and society, yet each ultimately fails to accomplish this. For Milkman in *Song of Solomon* and Jadine and Son in *Tar Baby*, the individual and community are brought closer, but still left apart and unreconciled. Yet in *Beloved* Morrison for the first time shows communal concerns and individual quests enabling and completing each other: Sethe's need to come to terms with her past is fulfilled only through the commu-nity's exorcism of the haunting presence of that past; and in that exorcism the community's own need to be reconciled with Sethe is fulfilled. This rec-onciliation is continued in *Jazz*, where the community forms the very voice that tells the tale of reconciliation that dominates the novel; and even *Par-adise*, which returns to a community that is predatory and destructive, suggests in its mystical close a possibility of healing and restoration. This progres-sion—from annihilation to regeneration, from victimization to reconcilia-tion—demands an interpretive response that can make sense of the shift in Morrison's narrative strategies and her creative vision.

If Morrison's central thematic concern is the relation between the indi-vidual and the community, her dominant aesthetic concern has always been that of the sublime. As the domain of the unspeakable, the unrepresentable, the awesome and awful, the transcendent, supernatural, and even inhuman, the sublime is the aesthetic realm that dominates Morrison's fiction. The unrepresentable horrors that lurk throughout her novels, the psychic and ontological fragmenting that disrupts her characters, and the constant effort to push the boundaries of language and the symbolic realm all indicate the dominance of the sublime in Morrison's work. But if her later writing indi-cates a shift away from these concerns, and a movement towards reconciliation and regeneration, then a different dominant aesthetic is needed to explain and account for this new direction. This different aesthetic is the aesthetic of the beautiful: long the contrary to the sublime, the beautiful offers a criti-cal vocabulary and an aesthetic structure that can interpret and account for the dramatic shift in Morrison's aesthetic, social, and ethical vision that is announced with *Beloved*.

It is appropriate that the sublime serves as the dominant aesthetic in a writer who has risen to prominence in the last three decades of the twenti-eth century; for during this so-called "postmodern" era the sublime has re-emerged as perhaps the definitive critical category. For theorists as diverse as

Jean-Francois Lyotard, Fredric Jameson, Harold Bloom, Neil Hertz, Paul de Man, and Ihab Hassan, the sublime serves to delineate the experiences of terror, fragmentation, and apocalypse that seem to define late twentieth-century art and culture. In particular, the annihilation of the self and the irrevocable disruption of the relation between the individual and the community are the hallmarks of what Bloom terms the "negative sublime." Hertz asserts that in the encounter with the sublime, "it is precisely the mind's unity that is at stake," and the result of this encounter is "thoroughgoing self-loss . . . [a] radical flux and dispersion of the subject" (58–59). For Jameson, this annihilation of the self is matched by the destruction of the social realm: the sublime moment, he states, is "an experience bordering on terror, the fitful glimpse, in astonishment, stupor, and awe, of what was so enormous as to crush human life altogether" (34). Such notions of the sublime, we will see, match the fates prescribed to many of Morrison's characters and communities.

These apocalyptic, destructive visions of the sublime seem at odds with the classic formulations of the sublime in such figures as Longinus, Burke, and Kant, which seem to define the sublime as an experience of transcendence, not devastation; and to be sure, one of the more remarkable shifts in twentieth century thought — beginning at least with Nietzsche, and accelerating in such thinkers as Heidegger, Kafka, and Conrad — has been the reconception of the sublime as an experience of destruction, not of transcendence. Nevertheless it was Burke who insisted that "terror is in all cases . . . the ruling principle of the sublime" (58); and Kant argued that in the sublime moment the imagination reaches a "point of excess . . . like an abyss in which it fears to lose itself" (107; see also Monk and Weiskel). The postmodern sublime only shifts the register of the experience: rather than contact with the divine, it depicts contact with the demonic; rather than a transcending of the human, it shows the destruction of the human. Its dominant voice, as Hassan asserts, is "the cry of outrage, the voice of apocalypse" (3). Such is precisely the aesthetic and narrative impulse of Morrison's writing all the way up to — and into — *Beloved*.

The aesthetic of the beautiful has hardly enjoyed the same surge in critical interest recently afforded to its contrary. Yet if Morrison's writing has shown a turn away from the sublime, its new concerns match with remarkable symmetry the tenets of the beautiful. The preservation of the individual self; the reconciliation between the individual and the community; the restoration and regeneration of the family, the home, and the natural world; and a powerful emphasis on *survival*, rather than destruction, are all contained within the principles of the beautiful. Burke and Kant each viewed the beautiful as a social principle; as Frances Ferguson has noted, both philosophers "link the beautiful with society and the sublime with individuals isolated [from society]," and define beauty as that which "draw[s] an individual into society" (3, 8). The tenuous, precarious, but nevertheless powerful tone of survival and hope that concludes *Beloved* and subtly pervades *Jazz* is precisely contained in Weiskel's summation of the essence of the beautiful: "The beautiful intimates reconciliation, however precariously and ambiguously" (48).

The shift from the sublime to the beautiful in Morrison's work carries aesthetic, ethical, political, and philosophical implications, all of which bear upon the complicated relationship between the individual and the community. Indeed, this dramatic shift in the aesthetic concerns of one of the most formidable writers of the late twentieth century suggests that a more rigorous and complex understanding of this relationship is needed. In this essay, I trace Morrison's aesthetic progression from the sublime to the beautiful — primarily in *The Bluest Eye, Song of Solomon,* and *Beloved,* though treating her other four novels as well — and show that this aesthetic development constitutes an unrelenting effort on Morrison's part to plumb the depths of the individual's place within the greater social realm, and the dangers and responsibilities inherent in this relation. Within this development, Morrison's goal throughout her writing remains consistent: to seek a way in which the individual can survive, and even flourish, within the larger boundary of the life-world.

The Bluest Eye presents the fundamental pattern of Morrison's early novels: an isolated figure, cut off from the community, must undergo a harrowing experience, an ontologically threatening encounter with what is variously described as the unspeakable, the otherworldy, the demonic — that is, the sublime. In the encounter with the sublime, these characters are excluded from a general gathering together of the community in beauty and harmony, and are condemned to fragmentation, psychosis, and death. In *The Bluest Eye,* Pecola Breedlove forms a peculiarly unstable core for the book. Pecola has no specified place, and she floats on the peripheries of the community she longs to enter. When Claudia Macteer is first informed by her mother that Pecola will be staying with them for a few weeks, she is told simply that "a 'case' was coming — a girl who had no place to go." Pecola has become homeless because her drunken father has destroyed their home, "and everybody, as a result, was outdoors" (17). This fear of being "outdoors" is "the real terror of life," a consuming anxiety about being without a fixed abode, without a house: "if you are outdoors, there is no place to go.... Outdoors was the end of something, an irrevocable, physical fact" (17–18). This fear of being homeless, radically unsettled, pervades Morrison's fiction. In *The Bluest Eye*, it defines the community's greatest fear, and also its relation to Pecola. For Pecola herself is constantly outdoors, never able to integrate herself into the community, always left on the peripheries, literally moving from house to house searching for a fixed place of comfort and security.

Pecola's position on the fringe of the black community is evident when she is taunted by a group of boys after school, in what Trudier Harris has described as "a rite of separation" in which "Pecola is given another opportunity to view her status as an outsider" ("Reconnecting Fragments" 72). Particularly painful because her own peers are excluding her, the jeers focus on Pecola's blackness and on her father's nakedness, prefiguring both her eventual rape by her father and also her desire to transform her blackness into what the novel posits as the essence of whiteness, the blond hair and bluest eyes of Shirley Temple. Claudia and Frieda's rescue of Pecola is only temporary, for soon Maureen turns on Pecola with the same taunt about her naked father. Pecola's reaction embodies her desire to vanish, to disappear in the face of a communal rejection she cannot bear: "Pecola tucked her head in— a funny, sad, helpless movement. A kind of hunching of the shoulders, pulling in of the neck, as though she wanted to cover her ears.... She seemed to fold into herself, like a pleated wing" (60–61).

This complex relationship between individual and community in *The Bluest Eye* is expressed through the ambiguous symbol of the house. The novel opens with the Dick and Jane primer that promises the idyllic home and family for which Pecola searches throughout the book: "Here is the house. It is green and white. It has a red door. It is very pretty. Here is the family. Mother, Father, Dick, and Jane live in the green-and-white house. They are very happy" (7). But as this chant is repeated in subsequent paragraphs, it becomes a frantic, unpunctuated stream of language without order, suggesting that behind this myth of a comforting, nurturing home lies a reality that is disordered and disrupting.

The house serves as the antidote to the evil of being outdoors, offering shelter and safety: "Knowing that there was such a thing as outdoors bred in us a hunger for property, for ownership. The firm possession of a yard, a porch, a grape arbor" (18). This desire for home is also a desire to curb the excess, the "funkiness," of the characters' lives: careful attention to boundary and limit will guard against the "dreadful funkiness of passion, the funkiness of nature, the funkiness of the wide range of human emotions" (68). The men seek a woman who has curbed her funkiness, for they know that such a woman will keep a house in which they will "feel secure" (68–69). But the home as haven is soon translated into the home as prison: "What they do not know is that this plain brown girl will build her nest stick by stick, make it her own inviolable world, and stand guard over its every plant, weed, and doily, even against him" (69). The house is simultaneously a respite and a jail; like the community, for which it stands as synecdoche, the house seems to promise rest and comfort, but it provides neither, especially for Pecola.

After her house is burned by her father, Pecola is twice attracted to other idyllic houses, only to be thrown out of them. When Pecola enters the home of a middle-class neighbor to see his kitten, she is struck by the order and comfort it offers: "How beautiful, she thought. What a beautiful house." But when the boy becomes sadistic and hurls the cat into the window, his mother immediately blames Pecola for disrupting her ordered home: "'Get out,' she said, her voice quiet. 'You nasty little black bitch. Get out of my house'" (73–75). Pecola, hurt and bewildered, is again turned outdoors as she leaves the house to face the cold wind and falling snow. The second incident occurs at the Fisher house, the white family's home where Pecola's mother, Pauline, works. Pauline is so enchanted by the "beauty, order, cleanliness" of the Fisher house that she "stopped trying to keep her own house," and instead "kept this order, this beauty, for herself, a private world" (100–101). Pauline views the Fisher house as the secure and splendid home that is denied her in her own life; she is unaware of its second aspect as a prison, unaware that the house, as the Fishers themselves say of Pauline, will "'never let her go'" (101). When Pecola comes to this house and nervously knocks a blueberry cobbler onto the kitchen floor, her mother strikes and curses her; while she comforts the Fisher daughter, Pauline shouts to Pecola to "'pick up that wash *and get on out of here*'" (87, emphasis added). Thus Pecola is for the third time thrown outdoors, and the house that—like the community as a whole, like Pecola's mother—promised such comfort and safety is transformed into a place of rage and fear, offering no haven for Pecola but only further confirming her isolation.

In this solitary and rejected state, Pecola wishes for the blue eyes that she feels will guarantee her love and acceptance; instead, she undergoes her father's delirium-induced rape of her. This is Pecola's harrowing experience, her contact with the unspeakable, what the book terms "a wild and forbidden thing" (128). Pecola's earlier efforts to disappear are re-enacted in an emptying-out of her spirit from her body, as "a hollow suck of air in the back of her throat" makes a sound like "the rapid loss of air from a circus balloon" (128). The malevolent aspect of the home is again emphasized here, for, as Madonne Miner points out, "Pecola's rape occurs within her own house, and this fact increases its raw horror" (88). Pecola is destroyed within her very community, and that community not only fails to aid her, they have helped cause her isolation.

Pecola's rape is the unspeakable horror at the center of Morrison's narrative, as indicated by the very inability of the community to tell the story coherently. The tale is communicated only in "fragments of talk" that must be "properly placed" in order "to piece a story together, a secret, terrible, awful story" (147). As Morrison has said, at the center of *The Bluest Eye* "is a terrible story about things one would rather not know anything about." The novel is built around a "Big Secret" that masks a terrible event: "A skip, perhaps, in the natural order of things." But this event, though described, nevertheless *resists representation*; the novel does not represent what Morrison describes only as "the silence at its center. The void that is Pecola's 'unbeing'" ("Unspeakable Things" 21–22). Hence at the very heart of the novel is a horrifying event in which representation fails—a manifestation of the sublime in its darkest aspect, fitting Lyotard's description of the sublime, that it "will enable us to see only by making it impossible to see" ("Answering the Question" 78). At the heart of *The Bluest Eye* is precisely such an inability to see, to give shape to an unspeakable truth that threatens and finally overwhelms Pecola.

That truth is revealed in the community's reaction to Pecola's trauma: they turn away from her, and deny the security and the welcome she has desired. Claudia and Frieda feel pity for Pecola, but are aware that no one else seems to share their feelings: "we listened for the one who would say, 'Poor little girl,' or, 'Poor baby,' but there was only head-wagging where those words should have been. We looked for eyes creased with concern, but saw only veils" (148). Indeed, the community is part of the very cause of Pecola's pathetic desire for blue eyes: sundered from her own people, denied acceptance into the only world she can know, Pecola is forced to try to reconceive herself as the most lovable, adored object she can imagine, the Shirley Temple doll. Morrison has stated that the reason for Pecola's desire must be at least partially traced to the failures of Pecola's own community: "she wanted to have blue eyes and she wanted to be Shirley Temple ... because of the society in which she lived and, very importantly, because of the black people who helped her want to be that. (The responsibilities are ours. It's our responsibility for helping her believe, helping her come to the point where she wanted that.)" (Stepto, "Intimate Things" 22).

Rather than offering a site for survival in a hostile and threatening world, the community in *The Bluest Eye* represents the very antithesis of survival: it rejects Pecola, and indeed drives her to the psychic disintegration she suffers by the novel's conclusion. Ruth Rosenberg suggests that survival in this novel is possible only to the extent that one *resists* the lure of the community: "Claudia's ability to survive intact and to consolidate an identity derives from her vigorous opposition to the colorist attitudes of her community" (440). Ultimately the relationship between the individual and the community in this novel is a vampiric one, with the community preying upon and sucking the very life out of the individual, making Pecola a sacrificial figure whose destruction guarantees the continued existence of the community: "All of us," Claudia states, "felt so wholesome after we cleaned ourselves on her. We were so beautiful when we stood astride her ugliness" (159).[3]

Pecola's fate in this novel is utter psychic fragmentation and disintegration: "the damage done was total" (158). Ravaged simultaneously by her contact with the unspeakable and by her community's rejection of her, Pecola is mentally shattered, consigned to a perpetual existence on the periphery, "on the edge of town" (159), outdoors forever. Miner describes her psychic damage as "of such an extreme that her very identity is called into question" (92). Pecola's fate is precisely the "ontological dislocation" that Lyotard sees as the essence of the experience of the sublime ("The Sublime" 12). Thus Morrison has stated that the central metaphor in the novel is "the visual image of a splintered mirror," an image that constitutes both "the form as well as the content of *The Bluest Eye*" ("Memory" 388).

The Bluest Eye concludes with Claudia's final meditation on Pecola's fate, in which she views the shattering of Pecola as part of an entire economy of sterility and death, which embraces as well the community and even the land itself: "it was the fault of the earth, the land, of our town. I even think now that the land of the entire country was hostile to marigolds that year. This soil is bad for certain kinds of flowers. Certain seeds it will not nurture, certain fruit it will not bear, and when the land kills of its own volition, we acquiesce and say the victim had no right to live" (160). The vision this novel offers, then, is a grim one: a virtually helpless individual—crucially, a child—is sundered from her community, and subsequently devastated through contact with the unspeakable. Not only does the community fail to aid her in her distress; they are ultimately shown to be complicitous in Pecola's destruction. And this destruction affects them as well, as all elements of this world, even the land itself, are consigned to an unregenerate death.

Song of Solomon also features an unstable central figure in Milkman Dead, a character who lacks character, a self without a strong sense of self. Breast-fed overlong by his clinging mother, overshadowed by his dominant father, Milkman finds it difficult to formulate his own ideas about himself or his world—"all he knew in the world about the world was what other people had told him" (120)—and this self-alienation is rooted in his alienation from his community. As Kathleen O'Shaugnessy has argued, "in the black community [Milkman] . . . is ultimately alienated from every group and individual with whom he comes in contact, particularly his family" (126). When he looks at his face in the mirror, Milkman finds that "it lacked coherence, a coming together of the features into a total self. It was all very tentative, the way he looked, like a man peeping around a corner of someplace he is not supposed to be, trying to make up his mind whether to go forward or to turn back" (69–70). Theodore Mason states that "Milkman's identity is a mass of fragments which never coheres into a whole" (573), and this isolation is simultaneously the cause and the effect of Milkman's status as a fragmented, incomplete figure.

As most critics read the novel, the progress of Song of Solomon consists in Milkman's gradual education in his past, his lineage, and his ties to his communal traditions: through learning where he comes from, Milkman arrives at an understanding of who he is. While trapped in his state of isolation, Milkman is prevented from seeing the very structures that will give him identity and strength; he is unable to attend to other stories besides his own: "the movement of the novel is marked by Milkman's progressive revelation that his persistent ignorance is a function of being locked inside his own story, sealed off from other people and other stories" (Mason 575). Yet this conventional reading of the novel as a steady progression towards reconciliation between the individual and the community is ultimately belied by the conclusion of the novel, a conclusion that leaves Milkman and his community as far apart as ever. And this separation is again marked by the sublime, by a haunting presence that intimates the truth of the failed relation between self and society.

As in *The Bluest Eye*, the key tensions of the novel are embodied in the images of the house. Milkman is torn between two competing visions of the house, one belonging to his father, Macon, the other to his aunt, Pilate. Milkman begins the novel immersed in the house of his father, unable to see his way out of his father's house despite his sense that his life there is isolated and fragmented; as the novel progresses, Milkman steadily departs from the way of life of his father, as he opens himself to the heritage of his past. This transformation of Milkman is enabled by the figure of Pilate, whose house offers Milkman the sense of community and belonging denied him in the rest of his life.

Macon Dead's "big dark house of twelve rooms" is the largest and finest black-owned home in town. Yet despite the physical finery of the home, many in the town "knew that the house was more prison than palace" (9–10). As in *The Bluest Eye*, behind the attractive veneer of the house lurks a malevolent and destructive interior. This dual aspect of the home finds its most powerful expression in *Song of Solomon* in the Butler House, the white ancestral home of the family who murdered and stole the land of Macon Dead, Sr. This house, which exhibits all the beauty and riches of a palatial mansion, contains only sterility, evil, and death. When Milkman enters he finds the ancient Circe and a pack of dogs inhabiting its ruined splendor, revealing the house as an image of the whited sepulchre in Matthew 24, appearing beautiful outward, but within full of dead men's bones and all uncleanness.[4] Macon rules his own home with an ethic of ruthless ownership; as he emphasizes to his son: "'Let me tell you right now the one important thing you'll ever need to know: Own things. And let the things you own own other things. Then you'll own yourself and other people too'" (55). Unlike Macon's father, who once claimed one of the finest farms in Pennsylvania's Montour County, Macon's relationship to property is not one of cultivation and generation, but one of extraction and sterile objectification. Yet despite his amassing of property and wealth, Macon is still unable to feel comfortable in his own house, which conjures images for him of his wife's "unyielding back," his daughters "boiled dry from years of yearning," and his son "to whom he could

the beginning of Milkman's education in the meaning of such terms: "Milkman smiled and let his shoulders slump a little. It was a good feeling to come into a strange town and find a stranger who knew your people. All his life he'd heard the tremor in the word: 'I live here, but my *people*...' or: 'She acts like she ain't got no *people*,' or: 'Do any of your *people* live there?' But he hadn't known what it meant: links" (229). As Milkman begins the exploration of his ancestral past, the sense of having a "people" begins to resonate more for him. Yet upon arriving in Shalimar, which Milkman expects to offer him the true home for which he has been searching, he is greeted instead with insults and knife blades: "He had thought this place, this Shalimar, was going to be home. His original home.... But here, in his 'home,' he was unknown, unloved, and damn near killed. These were some of the meanest unhung niggers in the world" (270). Milkman assumes that home is a simple matter of geography: get to the right location, and an authentic identity will fall into place. What he learns in Shalimar, however, is that his communal identity must be *earned*, that is, Milkman must undergo his own harrowing — in the older sense of being torn, lacerated, cut through — in order to find who he is and where he has come from. Smith rightly points out that in order to find himself Milkman must shed "his pretenses," "his wealth," and especially "the leaden trappings of materialism" that link him to his father's way of life, before he can be admitted to the Shalimar community (147).

Milkman begins to understand that the accoutrements of his former life will not help him in his quest when he goes on the bobcat hunt with the old men of Shalimar. "His watch and his two hundred dollars would be of no help out here," he thinks, "where all a man had was what he was born with, or had learned to use. And endurance. Eyes, ears, nose, taste, touch — and some other sense that he knew he did not have: an ability to separate out, of all the things there were to sense, the one that life itself might depend on" (277). On the hunt Milkman realizes that the men and the dogs are communicating with one another in a language he cannot understand, that, like Blake's ancient poets, they are communicating on a level somehow prior to language: "No, it was not language; *it was what there was before language. Before things were written down*" (278, emphasis added). When Milkman begins to attend to this mythic pre-language, when he tries "to listen with his fingertips, to hear what, if anything, the earth had to say," he senses Guitar behind him; he is able to fend off Guitar's attack; he is able to find his way back to the hunting party; and he finds himself suddenly in an authentic relation to the earth, one with the land, not alienated from it: "he found himself exhilarated by simply walking the earth. Walking it like he belonged on it; like his legs were stalks, tree trunks, a part of his body that extended down down down into the rock and soil, and were comfortable there — on the earth and on the place where he walked" (279–81).

Having endured such mythic trials as the fight and the hunt, Milkman is approaching a more authentic relationship with the people of his ancestral home. He comes to feel "connected" to these people, "as though there was some cord or pulse or information they shared. Back home he had never felt that way, as though he belonged to anyplace or anybody. He'd always considered himself the outsider in his family" (293). Significantly, this sense of communal attachment "reminded him of how he used to feel in Pilate's house." As Milkman grows closer to the Shalimar world, and as he begins to attend to the Solomon song that will prove to be the crucial link between his present and his past, he finds himself thinking more and more of Pilate and her home: "Milkman smiled, remembering Pilate. Hundreds of miles away, he was homesick for her, *for her house*" (300, emphasis added).

At this point, Milkman listens more closely to the children's song, and finding himself without pen or paper, is forced to memorize it orally, without the aid of written words. This continues Milkman's training in attentiveness, begun in the woods when he listens to the hunters' mythic pre-language. Upon hearing and deciphering the Solomon song, Milkman's relationship to his true, ancestral lineage becomes clear, and his relationship with the community in Shalimar is strengthened as well. This central event that frees Milkman from his previous state of isolation and fragmentation and brings him toward both self and communal awareness is an encounter with a language that defies representation. Both the hunters' communication and the children's song express "what was there before language," "before things were written down"; like the central event of Pecola's rape, these moments are precisely inexpressible — *they cannot be written.* And like Pecola's harrowing experience, this one too brings into relief the extent to which Milkman is estranged from his people. Yet unlike Pecola's encounter with the unrepresentable, Milkman's seems to be an event that heals and brings him towards understanding of himself and his world, rather than increases the gulf between them. Indeed, for Milkman the sublime *must* be encountered if he is to find himself.

The unrepresentable — what Morrison terms the "unspeakable" — plays a significant role throughout *Song of Solomon*, primarily through the presence

in the novel of ghosts and in the figure of Pilate. When Milkman asks him
to tell him about the ghosts, Freddie resists, saying, "'*I don't do no talkin 'bout
the ghosts I seen. They don't like that*'" (109, emphasis added). These haunting presences cannot be described; nevertheless, Freddie warns Milkman to
pay more attention to ghosts in order to understand the world around him.
Ghosts "appear" at crucial times throughout the novel: Pilate and Macon are
guided by the ghost of their father (141, 169–70); their father's ghost appears
to Pilate again when she is wandering alone (147); and a ghostly presence is
suggested when Milkman and Guitar steal the bag of bones from Pilate's
house (186). Indeed, the most prominent haunting figure in the book is the
ghost of Solomon, the original father who flew away generations before, but
whose presence determines the entire course of the novel. In addition, Pilate
is even more conspicuous in the role of unearthly presence: born without a
navel, evidence that she is not among those "'people who were born natural,'" Pilate is the unnatural, the extra-human "something God never made"
(143–44). Pilate's extraordinary nature serves to expand the horizon of the
possible in the novel, as Milkman himself observes just before hearing the
song of Solomon: "One fact was certain: Pilate did not have a navel. Since
that was true, anything could be, and why not ghosts as well?" (294).

Crucially, Pilate is the one who serves to open Milkman's consciousness
to the power and presence of the otherworldly, for precisely this openness
enables him to attend first to the chant of the hunters, and then to the children's song, the very elements that bring him towards understanding of himself and his world. Pilate serves as Milkman's guide, his pilot, a Charon figure who escorts him *to the other side*, beyond the realm of the earthly and the
merely human. For as Weiskel asserts, "The essential claim of the sublime is
that man can, in feeling and in speech, transcend the human" (3). This marks
Pilate as a literal vehicle for the sublime, for she effects the translation from
one state to another, across the threshold from the human realm to the extra-human. This is a definitive aspect of the sublime, whose very etymology
suggests a liminal experience, something occurring on the boundary or margin of human existence (see Arensburg, and also Cohn and Miles). Burke
himself emphasized the haunting characteristic of the sublime, its ability to
point towards an otherworldliness, a sense of the transcendent to which language can refer, but which language is powerless to represent.[5] Pilate is the
figure in *Song of Solomon* who effects this intimation of the otherworldly.

Through his relationship with Pilate and his attentiveness to otherworldly forms of communication, Milkman appears to be brought from his earlier state of isolation and fragmentation to a state of wholeness in himself and in his relation to his community. Certainly this is how most critics interpret the novel's conclusion: the stories Milkman absorbs in the south "enable him to feel a coherent, genuine sense of self as well as a profound commitment to others" (Smith 149). Just as Milkman reaches out to the community around him, so too does that community extend itself to Milkman: "the entire community of the rural Virginia town takes part in Milkman's discovery of his identity through the untangling of his past" (O'Shaugnessy 129). Once Milkman has discovered who he is and where he comes from, he is able to return to his hometown in Michigan with a sense of belonging and caring. Though he arrives too late to prevent Hagar's death, he assumes responsibility for her spirit, carrying her hair back to his father's house in place of the trappings of wealth with which he had left (334). As O'Shaugnessy points out, "although he cannot undo the past, he attempts to interact with the community he had had little part of before" (131).

Consequently, it would seem that Milkman is able to accomplish precisely what eludes Pecola: to move from a state of isolation to a state of both self and communal awareness. Yet the novel does not conclude with Milkman's return to his community in Michigan, but rather with his and Pilate's journey to Shalimar to bury Pilate's father, a burial that ends in Pilate's death and Milkman's jump from Solomon's Leap. There is something troubling in the fact that Milkman follows so exactly in the footsteps of his forefather. For whether Milkman flies or falls, his gesture is an echoing of the same abandonment of others that Solomon enacted generations before. When Milkman tells Sweet about Solomon's flight, she asks a question that Milkman seems hardly to regard: "'Who'd he leave behind?'" Milkman responds enthusiastically, "'Everybody! He left everybody down on the ground and he sailed on off like a black eagle'" (328). Heroic as Solomon's flight is, it nevertheless is emphasized throughout the novel that leaving kin behind is a sin that stays with a person, living or dead. When Pilate first converses with her father's ghost, she is admonished that "'you just can't fly on off and leave a body'" (147)—precisely what Milkman does in the novel's final gesture, thereby abandoning his crucial figure of translation and transmission. In this novel that is haunted by the figures of fathers who vanish—the flying Solomon, the murdered Jake, Guitar's father who is literally sliced in half, the absent fathers of Reba and Hagar—the closing image of this act of abandonment being repeated is at best ambiguous. As Morrison has stated, the flight of the fathers is admirable, "but there is a price to pay—the price is the children" (Watkins 46). By surrendering to the air, Milkman may or may not achieve the kind of transcendence his forefather achieved; regardless, the community he leaves behind cannot follow him, and so the relationship between individual and community which the novel is at such pains to construct is abandoned. Though the logic of the novel seems to propel the individual and the community back together, in the end that relationship breaks down, and they are left apart. A union between the individual and the community is envisioned, but it is left unattained.[6]

Beloved, Morrison's fifth novel, also focuses on an individual who is isolated from the community, and offers the strongest expression of any of Morrison's works of the harrowing experience the individual must undergo at the hands of, and in order to be reconciled with, the community. Yet *Beloved* is also the first of Morrison's novels to present a true union between individual and community in its conclusion, in which both self and society are regenerated and revived. This reconciliation is possible only through the encounter with the sublime, an encounter that both the individual and the community must undergo. By passing through this encounter, they emerge on the other side, as it were, in a new aesthetic domain: the realm of the beautiful.

Beloved begins precisely where Morrison's other novels end: with the individual and the community sundered. The community in *Beloved* has turned its back on Sethe and her family following Sethe's murder of her infant daughter, an ordeal severe enough to drive Sethe's mother-in-law, Baby Suggs, away from her position as community preacher and into her sickbed until she dies: "to belong to a community of other free Negroes—to love and be loved by them, to counsel and be counseled, protect and be protected, feed and be fed—and then to have that community step back and hold itself at a distance—well, it could wear out even a Baby Suggs, holy" (177). The community maintains its separation from Sethe because of her murder of her own daughter; but it first turns on her prior to this act. Angered and offended by the bounteous feast Baby Suggs offers on Sethe's arrival, the community fails to warn them about the slavecatcher's approach—the four horsemen ride straight through town, yet still take Sethe and her family by surprise (157). Hence, when Sethe takes her own daughter's life to prevent her being returned to the south, the community too shares part of the blame. When Sethe is led away, the community does not rally around her in spiritual kinship — rather, they allow her to be taken away utterly alone, without even the accompaniment of their music: "Was her head a bit too high? Her back a little too straight? Probably. Otherwise the singing would have begun at once, the moment she appeared in the doorway of the house on Bluestone Road. Some cape of sound would have quickly wrapped around her, like arms to hold and steady her on the way. As it was, they waited till the cart turned about, headed west to town. And then no words. Humming. No words at all" (152).[7] Consequently, the sin in this novel is both individual and communal; thus for any kind of forgiveness and reconciliation to occur, both the community and the individual must be included.

Once again, the symbol of the house embodies the separation of the individual and the community, as well as the haunting, uncanny forces that mark this sundering. *Beloved* opens with an address — "124 was spiteful. Full of a baby's venom" (3) — situating the house not only as the primary scene but also as the primary figure, in a sense the principal character. As Denver observes, the house functions as "a person rather than a structure. A person that wept, sighed, trembled and fell into fits" (29). This house is simultaneously sheltering and menacing: while it is "'just sad'" to Sethe, Paul D sees it as "'evil'" (8). Denver complains to Sethe that she cannot continue living in the house, because of the isolation it forces on them: "'I can't live here. I don't know where to go or what to do, but I can't live here. Nobody speaks to us. Nobody comes by'" (14). Denver longs for a place of refuge, a shelter where her loneliness will be eased. Her ring of boxwoods behind 124 serves this purpose for her, but it is clear that the house cannot provide this safety for Denver. As Paul D realizes, that "was exactly what was missing in 124: safety" (164).

Nevertheless, despite the menacing and haunting quality of 124, Sethe realizes that a house is a possession to be prized and not taken lightly. She dismisses Paul D's advice that she leave the house, "as though a house was a little thing — a shirtwaist or a sewing basket you could walk off from or give away any old time. She who had never had one but this one; she who left a dirt floor to come to this one" (22). As Morrison herself has stated, a house with an address was "a thrilling enough prospect for slaves who had owned nothing, least of all an address" ("Unspeakable Things" 31). Indeed, in *Beloved* — in contrast to *The Bluest Eye*, *Song of Solomon*, and *Tar Baby* — the house itself represents neither a positive nor a negative element in the novel; rather, the house is the *contested ground* over which the forces of the novel fight it out. As Denver realizes, the malevolent forces that compelled her mother to kill her sister are external to the house: "Whatever it is, it comes from outside this house, outside the yard, and it can come right on in the yard if it wants to. So I never leave this house and I watch over the yard, so it can't happen again and my mother won't have to kill me too" (205). Hence the house does serve as a refuge from these haunting forces; yet it is at the same time a prison, as Denver and Sethe are trapped within by "the voices that ringed 124 like a noose" (183).

The haunting presence that surrounds and eventually invades the house takes shape, of course, as Beloved, the literal embodiment of the ghost that has filled 124 since the murder of Sethe's daughter. From her first appearance — walking fully dressed out of the water, with "new skin, lineless and smooth" (50–52) — Beloved is a figure of the uncanny. As Sethe comes to realize, Beloved is a supernatural figure who has invaded the natural world; she is a figure "from the other side" (98). Pressed by Paul D to reveal where she came from, Beloved names a bridge as her place of origin (65), thereby emphasizing her nature as a liminal figure, a character who exists on the threshold between one world and another. As Susan Bowers has argued, Beloved herself functions as a bridge in this novel: "She herself becomes a bridge between the 'other side' and the living, the apocalyptic manifestation of the world beyond the veil. Like a bridge, Beloved enables passage to knowledge of the other side that otherwise would be impossible" (68). In short, Beloved is the figure of the sublime, offering in her very body intimations of the unrepresentable. Thus Beloved closely resembles Pilate, who is also an uncanny figure, apparently not born through human agency. Yet Beloved possesses a malevolence that Pilate never approaches, and this has much to do with the different direction taken at the close of *Beloved*.

This "knowledge of the other side" is the primal force that drives the novel. Whereas Baby Suggs preached an ethic of moderation and containment — " 'Everything depends on knowing how much,' she said, and 'Good is knowing when to stop' " (87) — Beloved represents the crossing of boundaries, excess and overflow. In her central monologue — a passage reminiscent of the increasingly chaotic language that opens *The Bluest Eye* — language becomes fragmented and disordered, unable to give coherent voice to the forces Beloved tries to express (210–13). These forces remain unrepresentable, "unspeakable thoughts, unspoken" (199). This is precisely how Lyotard describes the sublime, as the intimation of an idea "of which no presentation is possible," as a moment that "impart[s] a stronger sense of the unpresentable" ("Answering the Question" 78). As Beloved herself asks—suggesting a link with the sublime language intimated in *Song of Solomon*—"how can I say things that are pictures" (210). Beloved is, as Bowers points out, an apocalyptic figure, in the sense of apocalypse as "unveiling." She functions as "an apocalyptic demolition of the boundaries between the earthly and spiritual realms, an invasion of the world of the living by the world beyond the veil" (60). Again, this is the very function of the sublime according to Lyotard: "making reality increasingly ungraspable, subject to doubt, unsteady" ("The Sublime" 16). Beloved signifies the most ambitious attempt in Morrison's fiction to give representation to the unrepresentable.[8]

The double aspect of the house, as both comforting and malevolent, is mirrored in the figure of Beloved, who, in keeping with her sublime aspect, is both attractive and terrifying, appealing and overwhelming. This of course is the classic experience of the sublime: an experience of pleasure in the midst of pain, of exultation in the midst of terror. As Kant says of the manifestations of the sublime: "their aspect is all the more attractive for its fearfulness" (110–11). Beloved is simultaneously Sethe's lost child returned, and as such a figure of apparent forgiveness and reconciliation, and also an avenging demon, come to exact a price for Sethe's murder of her. This latter aspect increases as the novel nears its climax, and Beloved becomes vampiric, feeding on Sethe's spirit to augment her own strength. Denver observes that "the flesh between her mother's forefinger and thumb was thin as china silk and there wasn't a piece of clothing in the house that didn't sag on her"; meanwhile Beloved "was getting bigger, plumper by the day" (239). Eventually Sethe quits moving at all, except when tending Beloved: "The bigger Beloved got, the smaller Sethe became" (250).

Driven by starvation and the need to protect her mother from the voracious demon Beloved has become, Denver determines to leave the house and seek aid from the community. For Denver this decision is tantamount to leaping into a void: "She would have to leave the yard; step off the edge of the world. . . . she stood on the porch of 124 ready to be swallowed up in the world beyond the edge of the porch" (243). Denver fears that the community will devour her, fragment her much as Pecola was fragmented by her community; or that she will be rejected by the community, left, like Sula, to fend for herself in isolation. Certainly this is the pattern we might expect, based on Morrison's earlier novels. But instead the community embraces Denver, offering her help and giving her a sense of belonging that contrasts explicitly with the fate suffered by Pecola.

Denver goes to the home of Mrs. Jones, the schoolteacher she once knew. When Mrs. Jones hears of the troubles at 124, her response is immediate and sympathetic: "'Oh, baby,' said Mrs. Jones. 'Oh, baby'" (248). These are the very words that Pecola needed to hear, yet was denied: "But we listened for the one who would say, 'Poor little girl,' or, 'Poor baby,' but there was only head-wagging where those words should have been" (*Bluest Eye* 148). Mrs. Jones's response initiates Denver into the world of the community, but here—for the first time in Morrison's fiction—that community is nurturing, protective, and sheltering. This initiation brings Denver towards adulthood and responsibility: "She did not know it then, but it was the word 'baby,' said softly and with such kindness, that inaugurated her life in the world as a woman" (248). As Denver gains aid from the community and looks for work to save her household, she finds a sense of identity forming within her for the first time: "It was a new thought, having a self to look out for and preserve" (252).

Like her mother and Baby Suggs before her, Denver goes to the Bodwin family for employment. Their maid Janey remembers when Baby Suggs came to the same house with the same request: "'I've been here since I was fourteen,'" she says to Denver, "'and I remember like yesterday when Baby Suggs, holy, came here and sat right there where you are'" (253). Thus, like Milkman retreading the path of his ancestors, Denver, by following in the steps of her grandmother, enacts a rite of passage back into the community from which she and her family were sundered with the death of Beloved. Yet crucially, unlike the journey of Milkman, this rite of passage is completed, as Denver is embraced by the very community she seeks out. This also marks an explicit contrast with the fate of Jadine in *Tar Baby*, who fails to become integrated with her ancient community, and who instead "has forgotten her ancient properties" (305). Denver is able to overcome this sundering. Equally important, this makes the community aware of Beloved's reincarnated presence in 124. When Ella learns of Beloved's presence in the human world, she determines to take action to rid the community of the specter: "As long as the ghost showed out from its ghostly place—shaking stuff, crying, smashing and such—Ella respected it. But if it took flesh and came in her world, well, the shoe was on the other foot. She didn't mind a little communication between the two worlds, but this was an invasion" (257). The *actual presence* of Beloved is too much for Ella to bear. She gathers a company of thirty women and they march to 124 to exorcize Beloved from their midst. When they arrive, their chant reaches back towards the same mythic, pre-linguistic sound that the hunters gesture towards in *Song of Solomon*: "They stopped praying and took a step back to the beginning. In the beginning there were no words. In the beginning was the sound, and they all knew what that sound sounded like.... the voices of women searched for the right combination, the key, the code, the sound that broke the back of words" (259). This sound is precisely that which resists representation; it is a communication that transcends the coherence of language.

The effect of this chant upon Beloved is devastating. Curiously, Beloved is powerfully anxious about her body becoming fragmented and dispersed: "Among the things she could not remember was when she first knew that she could wake up any day and find herself in pieces. She had two dreams: exploding, and being swallowed" (133). Beloved — the figure of the sublime — expresses a primal terror that is precisely the terror *generated by* the sublime. As Weiskel explains, the anxiety generated by the sublime "is superimposed upon an original ambivalence ... a wish to be inundated and a simultaneous anxiety of annihilation" (105) — or as Beloved expresses it, a fear of either exploding or being consumed. In the face of the primal chant of the company of women, Beloved's anxieties are realized, as she undergoes her own dismemberment: "In the place where the long grass opens, the girl who waited to be loved and cry shame erupts into her separate parts, to make it easy for the chewing laughter to swallow her all away" (274).

Yet crucially, the rending undergone by Beloved — unlike that of, say, Pecola — is an event that *brings together* the individual and the community. David Lawrence points out that the chant of the women "creates communal bonds rather than destroying them"; in contrast to their prior abandonment of Sethe — and in contrast to the sunderings of Pecola, Sula, Milkman, Jadine and Son, from their communities — the community in this climactic scene "tries to sing Sethe back into its embrace" (197), claiming her as their own in a gesture that simultaneously saves themselves as well. For as Bowers argues, "when Sethe is taken back to the Clearing by the women's song in her yard, it is a sign of *both personal and community redemption*; the community at this apocalyptic moment has returned finally to loving themselves, but also to feeling compassion for those who have died" (72, emphasis added). Thus the individual enables the resuscitation of the community, just as the community enables the salvation of the individual. In this respect *Beloved* is a true apocalyptic narrative; "for although apocalyptic literature features the destiny of the individual and personal salvation, its 'overall perspective is still that of the community'" (Bowers 62).

After this sublime encounter, the house is stripped of its malevolent, imprisoning character. Paul D is able to return to 124, and finds that it is no longer haunted: "He looks toward the house and, surprisingly, it does not look back at him. Unloaded, 124 is just another weathered house needing repair" (264). Now neither prison nor palace, the house, as Stamp Paid attests, is quiet. Even Here Boy, the family dog, is able to return home, "so Paul D knows Beloved is truly gone" (263). With the sublime figure exorcised, the domestic realm is restored; and so the ongoing motif of the house in Morrison's fiction is finally resolved at the end of *Beloved*: what has been a representation of the hostility of the community becomes at last a site of stability, safety, and the merely human order of domesticity.

Paul D returns to Sethe and finds her emotionally exhausted and near despair following Beloved's exorcism. He recalls how Sethe "left him his manhood" when they were at Sweet Home, and attempts to return the gesture to her. Before Baby Suggs gave up her calling, she had told the community "that the only grace they could have was the grace they could imagine. That if they could not see it, they would not have it" (88). Paul D is the agent of such grace in this novel, as Sethe realizes when she looks at him "and sees it—the thing in him, the blessedness, that has made him the kind of man who can walk in a house and make the women cry. Because with him, in his presence, they could." Paul D "wants to put his story next to hers," an effort to join the two of them together that will allow them each to find their full sense of self-identity. "'You your best thing, Sethe. You are,'" Paul D tells her. Sethe responds, "'Me? Me?'"—an answer that implies a return to her self following her near-fatal encounter with Beloved.[9] As Barbara Schapiro points out, this closing gesture "suggests again an essential maintenance of boundaries, a balance of two like but separate selves, an attunement" (208). It is a turning away from the excess and overflow represented by Beloved and the sublime forces she embodied; a turning towards the cohesive and nurturing ideal of moderation, enabled by grace, preached by Baby Suggs.

lyptic conclusions that characterize so much of late twentieth-century fiction—one thinks of the conclusions of *Gravity's Rainbow, One Hundred Years of Solitude, Midnight's Children*—apocalypse in *Beloved* is a repeated event in a cyclical structure of time, which ushers in not annihilation, but renewal.[11] Rather than a destruction of both self and society, the apocalyptic chant of the women outside 124 is associated with revelation, transformation, and possibility: "*Beloved* proclaims that apocalypse and change are not necessarily at opposite poles: an apocalypse—that lifting of the veil on whatever lies beyond—can stimulate change. Its catharsis can be the beginning of transformation; apocalypse can thus become a bridge to the future, passage to freedom" (Bowers 67). The apocalyptic vision expressed in *Beloved* can perhaps best be characterized as apocalypse in the New Testament, rather than the Old Testament, sense, offering regeneration, not annihilation.[12]

Beloved is finally a novel about resisting the fragmenting, destructive energies of the sublime and turning instead to the conserving and regenerating energies of the beautiful. Bowers invokes this very language in her own summing up of the book: "*Beloved* is a novel about collecting fragments and welding them into beautiful new wholes, about letting go of pain and guilt, but also recovering what is lost and loving it into life" (74). *Beloved* is also the first of Morrison's novels in which the individual and the community are reconciled; and it is the novel in which the sublime is rejected most forcefully. Unlike Milkman's ambiguous leap towards transcendence, or Son's embrace of the mythic past that forsakes the present, *Beloved* concludes by consigning the sublime figure to oblivion: "By and by all trace is gone, and what is forgotten is not only the footprints but the water too and what it is down there. . . . This is not a story to pass on" (275). The new element in *Beloved* is precisely grace, the grace brought by Paul D and offered to Sethe, the "blessedness" within him that opens up the possibility of healing and regeneration. This is precisely what is lacking for Pecola, for Sula, for Milkman, for Jadine: a forgiveness that is neither earned nor deserved, but is nevertheless granted. That such an element may seem out of place in this "postmodern" era is exactly what makes Morrison's work so compelling at this very time.

Morrison has always been concerned with the relations between the past generations and the present: "The relationships of the generations have always been paramount to me in all of my works," she has stated, "the older as well as the younger generation, and whether that is healthy and continuing" (Ruas 103). In her efforts to explore the past and the present, the old and the young, Morrison has moved from depicting the failure of old and young—figured most powerfully in Cholly's rape of his own daughter—to the successful nurturing of old and young. Thus in her Nobel Lecture, Morrison depicts disgruntled and rebellious youth approaching an old, blind woman and asking her for wisdom, for guidance. The woman responds not with answers, orders, or directions, but with story, a story that the youths create with her: "'Look,'" she concludes, "'How lovely it is, this thing we have done—together'" (*Nobel Lecture* 13). If Morrison's primary aim as a novelist is to create something that is both beautiful and socially responsible, a work that both witnesses and also ministers to her people, then the aesthetic development of her writing indicates a frustration with her previous depictions and a desire to depict something new. This new depiction finally resolves into a meditation on love.

Beloved is reputed to be the first work in a trilogy that is all about love. This focus on love has really been the governing interest in *all* of Morrison's novels: as she has said, "all the time that I write, I'm writing about love or its absence" (Bakerman 40). But the conclusion of *Jazz,* with its celebration of the "public love" of "grown people" (228), indicates the distance traveled by Morrison in her study of human love:

It's nice when grown people whisper to each other under the covers. Their ecstasy is more leaf-sigh than bray and the body is the vehicle, not the point. They reach, grown people, for something beyond, way beyond and way, way down underneath tissue.... Breathing and murmuring under covers both of them have washed and hung out on the line, in a bed they chose together and kept together... and the mattress, curved like a preacher's palm asking for witnesses in His name's sake, enclosed them each and every night and muffled their whispering, old-time love. (228)

Crucially, this is a love that is experienced by, and even told by, the community itself: the nameless, faceless, disembodied narrator of *Jazz*—a persona who knows more than any one person could possibly know and who cares so deeply for the people whose stories the novel tells—can only be a plurality of voices, a blending of the many faces and names that constitute the community as a whole (see Conner, "Wild Women and Graceful Girls" 354–55). This choral voice concludes the novel with a paean to a love that is nurturing, healing, forgiving, and passionate.

Paradise is, along with *Beloved*, the most innovative and daring of Morrison's novels. Though its depiction of a community that preys upon its own young, its own women, and those outside of its narrow confines seems in some respects to return to the war between self and society depicted in Morrison's earlier work — indeed, *War* was Morrison's working title for the book ("This Side of Paradise") — nevertheless the novel reveals a continuation of the direction announced with *Beloved* and continued in *Jazz*. In her depiction of a community that is isolated, fearful, and hating of all that is outside of its narrow confines, Morrison reveals the devastation that hatred and isolation wreak upon their perpetrators. If *Beloved* examines the glories and the excesses of mother-love, and *Jazz* the glories and excesses of human love, *Paradise* shows the glories and excesses of love of God. The devastation caused by such an obsessive love serves as a warning — a "parable," as one critic has described the novel (Storace 64) — that the proper sphere of love is precisely the human sphere, the very sphere set forth in the first two novels of the trilogy.

Thus Morrison's work reveals an aesthetic progression that is simultaneously ethical as well. This progression is defined by a cohesive and nurturing sense of love, which Morrison herself has stated is the best, perhaps only, hope for healing a devastated world: "Love," she has stated, is the metaphor most in need today: "We have to embrace ourselves" (Moyers 266). Thus Morrison's work is an ongoing and passionate effort at healing the divisions that quite literally haunt the scarred individuals and fractured communities of late twentieth-century America; it is an effort to heal sublime wounds and to constitute beautiful worlds.

NOTES

1. It is far more difficult to find Morrison essays that do *not* mention the community than those that do; but representative examples of community-oriented scholarship include Christian; Cynthia A. Davis; Grant; O'Shaugnessy; Mason, Jr.; Mbalia; and Bjork.

2. Significant exceptions include Rosenberg and Trudier Harris. That both of these essays deal with *The Bluest Eye* suggests that Morrison's critique of community is strongest in this first novel, and becomes more subtle in her subsequent work.

3. In this respect Pecola is akin to Sula, who also functions as a scapegoat figure against whom the community can constitute itself: "Their conviction of Sula's evil changed them in accountable yet mysterious ways. Once the source of their personal misfortune was identified, they had leave to protect and love one another. They began to cherish their husbands and wives, protect their children, repair their homes and in general band together against the devil in their midst" (117–18). Of course, in Sula's case her scapegoat status is chosen and willed, whereas for Pecola it is forced upon her and resisted.

4. This idea of the house as whited sepulchre—a motif that links Morrison's work with several prominent American precursors, especially Faulkner, Hawthorne, and Poe—recurs throughout Morrison's fiction, most notably in Valerian Street's attempt at an Edenic island paradise in *Tar Baby*. Described initially as "a wonderful house...'the most handsomely articulated and blessedly unrhetorical house in the Caribbean'" (11), the home appears even to Son as "a safe port" (135). But as the terrible secret of the novel is revealed, the home is transformed into "a house of shadows" (235), and by the novel's end it has become Valerian's prison, overrun by ants and falling into disrepair.

5. See the enigmatic final section of Burke's *Enquiry*, "Of Words," where he discusses the haunting power of words that give the reader "no clear idea," but which "affect the mind *more than the sensible image would*" (174, emphasis added).

6. In this respect the novel resembles the conclusion of Morrison's next book, *Tar Baby*, in which Son seems to join the mythic tribe of "one hundred black men on one hundred unshod horses [who] rode blind and naked through the hills and had done so for hundreds of years" (206). Yet in so doing Son leaves behind Jadine, and any possibility of merging his own mythic destiny with her twentieth-century existence. The hope of a union and communal gathering in any real, pragmatic sense is left highly ambiguous at the novel's close, as Son retreats into a solitary, isolated existence.

7. This withholding of their song by the community recalls Sula's burial, when only a few people gather, and then they sing "Shall We Gather at the River" only "for politeness' sake" (150).

8. Though Beloved functions as the *embodiment* of the unspeakable, it should be emphasized that she is not identified as its *source*. One tempting location of the source of the avenging rage she represents is, of course, slavery itself; as Bowers argues, Beloved "is the embodiment of the collective pain and rage of the millions of slaves who died on the Middle Passage and suffered the tortures of slavery.... The invasion of the world of the living by Beloved's physical presence is evidence of the terrible destruction of the natural order caused by slavery" (66). To be sure, the link between the evils of slavery and the supernatural eruption depicted in the novel is indisputable; yet the straightforward correspondence of this eruption with a human institution, however peculiar, would be ultimately reductive. The sublime power Morrison depicts resists mere human identification.

9. This is one of the most powerful correlations between *Beloved* and the novel that follows it, *Jazz*. For *Jazz* also depicts fragmented selves (such as the "cracks" and "dark fissures" that compose Violet [22]); individuals sundered from home, family, and community (Joe Trace's restless efforts to find "that home in the rock" that is simultaneously womb, mother-love, and primal home [221]); and intimations of apocalypse ("the commencement of all sorts of destruction" [9]). But *Jazz* moves powerfully towards a concluding mood of reconciliation and regeneration that clearly matches that of *Beloved*, and offers a sense of restored self that Felice in particular imbibes from the older Joe and Violet: "'The way she said it. Not like the "me" was some

tough somebody, or somebody she had put together for show. But like, like somebody she favored and could count on. A secret somebody you didn't have to feel sorry for or have to fight for'" (210). For a detailed discussion of *Jazz* in terms of its aesthetic structure, its relation to Morrison's previous novels, and particularly its relentless movement toward regeneration, see Conner, "Wild Women and Graceful Girls."

10. See Rorty's two powerful essays discussing the "postmodern debate" between Lyotard and Jurgen Habermas, which Rorty describes as precisely a debate between an aesthetics of the sublime and an aesthetics of the beautiful: "Cosmopolitanism without Emancipation: A Response to Jean-Francois Lyotard," and "Habermas and Lyotard on Postmodernity."

11. For a detailed discussion of the postmodern sublime in Pynchon's writing, and the similar turn towards the aesthetic of the beautiful in his mature work, see Conner, "Postmodern Exhaustion." That both Pynchon and Morrison—arguably the two most significant American novelists of the post-World War II period—show a similar shift away from the apocalyptic sublime and towards the regenerative energies of the beautiful suggests a broader cultural shift in which each author is somehow participating.

12. In this respect, Morrison's aesthetic vision closely resembles that of Joyce in *Finnegans Wake*, a work marked by an almost comical number of apocalypses which serve not to bring life to an end, but rather to initiate a new cycle of life that builds upon and repeats that which came before. This suggests that Morrison's work is finally closer in many respects to her modernist precursors, rather than her "postmodernist" contemporaries. For forceful arguments in favor of Morrison's "modernist" associations, see Cowart, and Conner, "Wild Women and Graceful Girls."

TONI MORRISON'S
BEAUTY FORMULA

Katherine Stern

"The concept of physical beauty as a *virtue*," Toni Morrison wrote in 1974, "is one of the dumbest, most pernicious and destructive ideas of the Western world, and we should have nothing to do with it" ("Behind the Making" 89). Morrison was responding to the slogan "Black is Beautiful" which she took to be "a white idea turned inside out" that still reduced the worth of a people to their bodily appearance. "Concentrating on whether we are beautiful," she wrote, "is a way of measuring worth that is wholly trivial and wholly white and preoccupation with it is an irrevocable slavery of the senses" (89). However much beauty matters to white people, she added, "it never stopped them from annihilating anybody" (89).

Morrison's impatience with the very idea of physical beauty will be familiar to readers of *The Bluest Eye*, where the narrator calls beauty one of "the most destructive ideas in the history of human thought" and tells how Pauline

I would like to thank five colleagues who had a hand in this work. Elaine Scarry encouraged me to audit her seminar "On Beauty" at Harvard University where we read philosophical, literary, and scientific accounts and discussed their ethical implications, particularly the question of whether beauty can save an object from harm (Scarry 24–28, 66–67) and how beauty exerts a "pressure toward the distributional" (67, 80–81). Geraldine Johnson shared her research on the status of touch and vision in Renaissance aesthetic debates. Mary Hamer listened to early versions and offered many helpful suggestions. Sarah McNamer and Robert Zimmerman took their pencils to the final drafts, leaving me not only revised but touched.

Breedlove "was never able, after her education in the movies, to look at a face and not assign it some category in the scale of absolute beauty" (113). In a piece for the *New York Times Magazine* in 1971, Morrison wrote that it might be just as well for black women "to remain useful" rather than to strive for a more decorative status. The "romanticism" of beauty worship seemed to her "a needless cul-de-sac, an opiate" that "eventually must separate us from reality" ("What the Black Woman Thinks" 15).

Morrison's response to "the whole business of what is beauty and the pain of that yearning" (Ruas 95) seems unequivocal in the 1970s. Yet she continues to delineate the problem in *Song of Solomon*, *Tar Baby*, and particularly *Jazz*, while searching out ways to conceive beauty differently. As she later tells an interviewer, "A good cliché can never be overwritten; it's still mysterious. The concepts of beauty and ugliness are mysterious to me" (Tate 159–60). What novelistic practices does Morrison invent to counteract entrenched notions of beauty? How does she avoid the aesthetic impairment of categories, scales, and standards when she evokes her characters' features or describes their attractions to each other? How does she portray the beauty of the body so as to point to something mysterious rather than tedious? As her broad allusions to the "ideas of the Western world" and "the history of human thought" suggest, the attempt to recharacterize beauty necessarily pits her against a long-standing philosophical tradition.

Critics have been fascinated by Morrison's treatment of the "destructive, devaluing power of white standards of beauty" (Guerrero 768; see also McKay, "Introduction," and Somerville), but few have tried to describe the alternative approach to beauty that she offers. Some have suggested that Morrison develops a "black-defined standard of beauty" (Ashe 580) or "her own African-American standard" (Walther 783), based on "traditional beauty and strengths" (Denard 175), but the very notion of standards, as if for a beauty contest, seems to follow the reductive "Black is Beautiful" model, which excludes those with untypical or non-traditional black features while underestimating the problem of specularity itself—that is, the power of the visual to enslave or numb the other senses, subsuming other aspects of experience (Walther 775).

In this essay, I show how Morrison draws our attention away from the visual, the static, the remote, or idealized object, towards an experience of physical beauty that is tangible and improvisational, relational and contextual, involving mutual efforts to feel as well as see. Morrison does not merely circumvent Western aesthetic standards, but invents entirely original ways to approach the beautiful as work or process. In her narratives, beauty depends on the beholder's craft or intention and results from labor upon the body either by the hands or the imagination. What kinds of scenes and strategies allow Morrison to reconceive of beauty in this way? Oddly enough, the very aspect of culture that Morrison first condemns—the beauty industry—increasingly provides the cultural scene through which she finds her way out of seeing and into a beauty mediated by touch and fantasy.

In the course of this essay, I will first consider the variety and subtlety of Morrison's references to cosmetic ritual, showing how they convey her interest in the power to bestow beauty and her sense of the importance of agency— her recognition, even as a child, that "beauty was not simply something to behold; it was something one could *do*" ("Afterword" 209). I will then briefly point to the social and economic contexts of the African American beauty industry to explain why that primarily positive heritage would foster Morrison's approach to beauty through the category of the cosmetic. From there, I will move beyond the specific theme of cosmetics to consider more closely the faculties of perception that Morrison foregrounds in her portrayals of cosmetic acts. Morrison is fascinated by how the imagination comes to bear on the sense of touch to produce or stage beauty. She invents scene after scene in which these two aspects of aesthetic response, touch and imagination, conspicuously oppose or counter-balance the visual and objective tendencies of western thinking about beauty. However, Morrison's shift of attention to the tactile and imaginary does not serve merely to evade the problems of visual beauty, nor to retreat from the question of whether beauty ever saved anyone from annihilation. Rather, as I try to show at the end of the essay, her "beauty formula" seems to define a necessarily ethical and inclusive response to human bodies, one that extends tenderness to every person and precludes doing harm.

In the early novels, cosmetics provide the fulcrum for Morrison to explore both sides of the pernicious yet mysterious concept of beauty. On the one hand, Pecola's desperate longing for blue eyes and Hagar's maniacal shopping spree in *Song of Solomon* (314–18) are portrayed as self-destructive, even nihilistic impulses, expressing the wish, "Please, God, make me disappear" (*Bluest Eye* 44). Indeed, Hagar's death follows so closely on her bid to win back Milkman with new clothes and new makeup that her purchases—Maidenform, Sunny Glow and Mango Tango—seem to blame. Their false promises magnify Milkman's betrayal and deliver the final blow. Yet, at the same time, these excruciating, ill-fated makeover scenes hold out an intriguing possibility: that physical beauty really is no less than what Pecola and Hagar take it to be — a dire necessity that must somehow be reclaimed. We glimpse the possibility of that reclamation with the portrait of The Maginot Line, one of the magnificent "whores in whores' clothing" in *The Bluest Eye*, whose heavily made-up eyes look to Claudia like "waterfalls in movies about Hawaii" (73). Cosmetic rituals in the early novels express not only the danger of received notions of beauty, but also the characters' persistent yearning to have agency in conferring beauty on themselves. And even the most absurdly comic rituals demonstrate this relentless determination, as when Nel's mother scolds, "'Don't just sit there, honey. You could be pulling your nose'" (*Sula* 28).

In *Jazz*, we find a whole kaleidoscope of cosmetic ambitions and obsessions. As one reviewer describes, the characters "are all trying to change the way they look, or in business to change the way somebody else looks, even with a knife" (Leonard 716). Joe Trace carries a sample case of Cleopatra products door to door, while his wife Violet, unlicensed hairdresser, tries to get her hips back with Dr. Dee's Nerve and Flesh Builder. Joe meets his lover Dorcas while delivering "#2 Nut Brown and vanishing cream to Malvonne's cousin Sheila at Alice's social" (68), and when Joe shoots Dorcas, Violet shows up at the funeral to disfigure Dorcas's face. Later, Violet decides to "love — well find out about" Dorcas — "what kind of lip rouge the girl wore, the marcelling iron they used on her" (5) — and fantasizes about trimming Dorcas's hair (15, 109). Meanwhile Joe still thinks about Dorcas's "sugar-flawed" skin, how "a quart of water twice a day would have cleared it right up" (130), and Rose's husband carries Frieda's Egyptian Hair Pomade in his pocket along with "bottles of rye, purgative waters and eaux for every conceivable toilette" (100).

In surveying the whole panoply of beauty products and professionals in *Jazz*, we can see that Morrison separates off her critique of white beauty standards and the worship of beauty as an abstract ideal from the fascinating and diverse cosmetic efforts into which the characters draw each other. But Morrison's novels bear constant reminders of African-Americans' particular relation to beauty *work* — beauty as commerce, as service, something manufactured and exchanged. Even before *Jazz*, the self-satisfied air with which China, Poland, Miss Marie, or Nel's grandmother put on their makeup conveys something coded and complex and not entirely negative about cosmetic culture — something that is ultimately related to Morrison's project of reconnecting physical beauty to agency, and of exploring the mystery *and* usefulness of beauty work.

Morrison's unusual focus on cosmetics as a way of exploring women's agency can be explained, at least in part, by the particular historical relation that cosmetics have had to black women's community organizing and empowerment. In the early part of the twentieth century, black women encountered the commodification and popularization of beauty culture at the same time that they were first able to offer the work of grooming and beautifying to each other instead of to whites. Before the twentieth century, few black women had the privilege of performing such intimate and leisurely domestic labor as hair-dressing (Eliza Potter, who worked in Paris and London before settling back in Cincinnati with a large clientele of white women, was a notable exception; see Potter 1859, 1991). Fewer still were situated where they could serve other black women as "fancy hair-dressers"—in 1865, the *New York Citizen* recommends "the Misses Mahans of Thompson street near Spring" as the "creme de le creme of sable artists in wool" (Middleton Harris 190). But the first decade of the twentieth century saw an explosion of beauty products and services, especially hairdressing, designed by and for black women.

Annie J. Turnbo Malone, who created the Poro system of products in 1900, Sarah Spencer Washington, who started the Apex company in 1919, and Madam C. J. Walker, who invented and popularized hair-straightening with a heated iron comb and pomade, were among the first African Americans to start their own businesses and trade schools, employ tens of thousands of other women, and gain international recognition for their business savvy as well as philanthropy (see Bundles, Marianna Davis, Peiss, *Hope in a Jar*, and Porter). It may be overstating the case to suggest, as one of their biographers puts it, that they "belong to the hall of the immortals" where "their names will be whispered in terms of Love, Inspiration and Hope" (Porter 47), or that, as Henry Louis Gates, Jr. jokes, "it's a wonder we don't have a national holiday for Madame C. J. Walker...rather than for Dr. King" (*Colored People* 45). But it is hardly possible to overestimate the significance of the black beauty industry in the 1920s or the intense anxieties and aspirations it channeled.

When Morrison notes in the early pages of *Jazz* that "the hair of the first class of colored nurses was declared unseemly for the official Bellevue nurse's cap" (8), we get a sense of what the novel's hairdressers and cosmetics salesmen are working against; of what complex pressures, hopes, and rejections bore upon the makeup and hairstyles of 1920s Harlem, sandwiched as people were between the persistent dehumanization of racism and the aggressive marketing of beauty products. In 1928, Madam Walker's company ran a full-page newspaper advertisement with the headline: "Amazing Progress of Colored Race — Improved Appearance Responsible" (Peiss, "Making Faces" 156).

Morrison seems to question the good offices of Madam Walker, née Sarah Breedlove, when she bestows the ironic name Breedlove on Pecola and her family. Did the famous beautician and the industry she founded breed love or breed self-hate? Did Madam Walker's injunction to "Learn to Grow Hair and Make Money" breed self-confidence or insecurity? While the early novels testify to the harmful effects of the beauty industry, and Morrison's sole direct reference to Madam Walker sounds derisive — she has commented that "the assumption about our loving white folks is based on Madame Walker's success" ("Behind the Making of the Black Book" 87) — nevertheless, the lost "Palace of Cosmetology" evoked at the beginning of Sula holds some enduring fascination for Morrison. By the time she writes Jazz, her interest in cosmetic culture has turned toward its positive social and aesthetic value.

Scholars are now suggesting that, overall, the black beauty industry championed "culturally discrete symbols and practices" (Rooks 49), and fostered social networks and bonding rituals among black women. Beauty parlors and kitchens where women gathered and door-to-door sales to friends and neighbors "enhanced the web of mutual support and assistance integral to black women's culture" (Peiss, "Making Faces" 157). Many women have written in retrospect about the positive sense of community and nurturing they derived from the ostensibly oppressive experience of hair-straightening. Andrea Benton Rushing remembers the religious aura of the "biweekly transformation rituals" (331), and bell hooks evokes the female bonding experience: "This is our ritual and our time. It is a time without men. It is a time when we work to meet each other's needs, to make each other beautiful in whatever way we can" ("From Black is a Woman's Color" 382; see also "Straightening Our Hair"; see Willi Coleman, and also Cleage, who offers an alternative reading of the hair experiences).

Examining closely Morrison's choice of detail in Jazz, we find that she too writes about cosmetic acts more as occasions for contact and commerce among people than as occasions for looking ("'That's my ear, girl! You going to press it too?'" (14)). The beauty "experts" in Jazz offer their services out of a longing for connection: "One thing, for sure.... the girl needed her ends cut.

Hair that long gets fraggely easy. Just a quarter-inch trim would do wonders, Dorcas. Dorcas" (15). Morrison is shifting our attention from the abstract ideals to the material practice of beauty, from the category of the beautiful to the category of the *beautified,* and in so doing, she counteracts a fundamental Judeo-Christian prejudice against acknowledging the body as an artifact of fashion, its status as a product of cultural convention and creativity, rather than divine will. By drawing us into the mind of a hair-dresser, investing her labor with fine distinctions, Morrison shows cosmetic work as the means to experience physical beauty rather than to falsify it, and thus she challenges the essentialist notion of beauty as inborn, original, untouched or un-self-conscious virtue. But more than that, in passages such as the encomium on the Comfy Shampoo at a proper beauty parlor (18), the Shampoo becomes the *mise-en-scène* of a different, non-visual aesthetic based on tactility—the instinct to groom, to soothe, to "warm toward a touch" (note Morrison's use of this phrase in "Mercy"). Morrison is opening up alternate routes to the beautiful, specifying the diverse senses through which beauty reaches us, other than the visual. In other words, she is not so much interested in sociology as in aesthetics (Peterson, " 'Say make me remake me' " 201–21). There is a fascinating history that Morrison allows us to glimpse through her characters' cosmetic obsessions, but the glimpses are crafted so as to suggest new ideas about how and when beauty happens. Reminding us that paints and pomades and concoctions such as Nu-Nile provide pretexts for touching and soothing, Morrison points to the way that beauty is conferred by the laying on of hands.

Morrison's emphasis on the tactile over the visual conveys an implicit challenge to the western aesthetic fascination with sight and the corresponding degradation of touch. Aristotle considered touch the most lowly, animalistic sensation (*Nichomachean Ethics* 176–79) and Renaissance theorists echoed him. To Vincenzio Borghini, touch seemed "bestial" compared to sight, "the most crude and most material" of the senses (637). Leon Battista Alberti chose as his emblem a winged eye, explaining that the eye was an obvious symbol of supremacy, "more powerful than anything, swifter, more worthy.... It is such as to be the first, chief, king, like a god of human parts" (Summers 38). And Leonardo da Vinci in his *Treatise on Painting* declares that the eye "counsels and corrects all the human arts" and that "its sciences are most certain" (23).

In general, the discourse of aesthetics has endowed the visual faculty with objectivity, autonomy, and hence, dominion. Because visual sensation covers remote distances, its reach is considered lordly and authoritative, whereas tactile sensation, limited to the local and specific, seems lowly by comparison. Yet philosophers in the European tradition have at times been drawn to the very difficulty of describing the neglected, underestimated domain of touch. If in the *Ethics* Aristotle designates touch the most bestial and demoralizing of sense-pleasures, in *De Anima* he struggles to define this most diversified and diffuse of the senses, acknowledging that it has the "least obvious" location: "It is difficult to say whether touch is one sense or more than one, and also what the organ is which is perceptive of the object of touch; whether it is flesh ... or whether this is only the medium, and the primary sense organ is something distinct and internal" (*On the Soul* 129). Aristotle goes on to describe the way that touch involves both direct contact with an external stimulus and the sensation of a message conveyed from the surface of the body to some place further within, illustrating the ambiguity of the flesh's role with the metaphor of a man "wounded through his shield": "[T]here is a difference between tangible things, and visible or audible things. We perceive the latter because some medium acts on us, but we perceive tangible things not by a medium, but at the same time as the medium, like a man wounded through his shield; for it is not the stricken shield that struck him, but both he and the shield were struck simultaneously. ... From this it is clear that that which is perceptive of what is touched is within" (*On the Soul* 133).

The paradoxical immediacy and yet internal remove of touch reveals the dimensionality of the body's sensations, and this very depth perception, as Aristotle's choice of metaphor indicates, tends to disarm and overwhelm the subject. Diderot, in his "Letter on the Deaf and Dumb," writes that "of all the senses the eye [is] the most superficial ... touch the profoundest and the most philosophical" (45; see Jay, *Downcast Eyes* 101). The reach of touch is inward-going, then, its dominion internal. Touch has a certain intriguing complexity, according to both Aristotle and Diderot, that unsheathes the self's layers.

When Morrison explores the aesthetics of touch, she connects tactility to reciprocal, reflexive sensations, liberating the aesthetic not only from the visual as such, but from what Michele Wallace calls "the problem of the *autonomy* of the visual sphere" (224–25). Simply by describing a manicure, for example, Morrison has us reconceive beauty as dependent upon cooperative efforts: "[S]he has pushed back his cuticles, cleaned his nails and painted them with clear polish. ... She likes to know that the hands lifting and turning her under the blanket have been done by her. Lotioned by her with cream from a jar of something from his sample case" (*Jazz* 38–39). In a few sentences that shift from love-making to manicuring while Dorcas shifts from doer to done-to and back again, Morrison conveys not only the sharing of sensations but the sequentiality of touch, the way in which the other's touch, unlike the other's gaze, does not seem to occur simultaneously with one's own sensation, but by a lingering, alternating process. According to Merleau-Ponty this "ambiguous set-up" pertains even when the two hands touching are one's own: "When I press my two hands together, it is not a matter of two sensations felt together... but of an ambiguous set-up in which both hands can alternate the roles of 'touching' and being 'touched'" (93). The mutuality of touch takes time to register; the sensation itself has a narrative structure that invites the novelist's attention.

We might want to compare Morrison's emphasis on handiwork with Booker T. Washington's in *The Work of the Hands*, where he describes his first experience of gardening with the same kind of awe at the power to generate beauty that Morrison evokes in her accounts of manicuring or hair-styling. Giving a lawn "a clean-up" with a hand-scythe and surveying the pleasing results, Washington discovers "a self-respect, an encouragement and a satisfaction" that he had "never before enjoyed or thought possible" and "inspirations and ambitions which could not have come in any other way"; "I found myself, through this experience, getting rid of the idea which had gradually become a part of me, that the head meant everything and the hands little," he writes (9–10). But Morrison's attention to handiwork is distinct from Washington's in that she is primarily concerned with the head's experience; she is not so interested in surveying the actual work as she is in the mental images that are formed as a result. In *Paradise*, when Connie invites Mavis to help her shell a thirty-two-quart basket of pecans with the pointed expression, "make yourself useful," Mavis refuses until Connie re-imagines her hands for her, persuading her that beauty and usefulness are one and the same: "'Look at your nails. Strong. Curved like a bird's. Perfect pecan hands. Fingernails like that take the meat out whole every time. Beautiful hands, yet you say you can't'" (42). The speech is a revelation for Mavis. Beauty occurs to her, and in her, at that moment and she is persuaded, perhaps because she has been warmly praised, or perhaps because she sees for the first time her fingertips' cunning fitness in form to the pecans in their shells. Her hands now correspond to bird's claws, pecans—and with this new image of their purposiveness in mind, Mavis watches her "suddenly beautiful hands moving at the task" and revels in their "economy" and "grace." The scene exemplifies Washington's point about the beauty of usefulness, but goes a step further, showing that *imagining* handiwork, merely conceiving of it, gives rise to pleasure and reconnects Mavis to the material world. Whether she ever gets through all thirty-two quarts is beside the point.

If the cosmetic scenes in Morrison's fictions materialize beauty by insistently portraying the handiwork involved, they also spiritualize beauty by drawing attention, as the pecan-shelling scene does, to the imagination's part in elaborating the handiwork, supplementing it with an idealized double. A brief glimpse of China's "getting ready" in *The Bluest Eye* makes this distinction between the actual and imagined results of beauty work comically obvious: "China had changed her mind about the bangs and was arranging a small but sturdy pompadour. She was adept at creating any number of hair styles, but each one left her with a pinched and harassed look. Then she applied makeup heavily. Now she gave herself surprised eyebrows and a cupid-bow mouth. Later she would make Oriental eyebrows and an evilly slashed mouth" (56). The passage works out emphatically, in miniature, the distinction Morrison makes throughout *The Bluest Eye* between the impact of an optical, external effect and an imagined one. For just as Pecola's internal images eventually overwhelm her powers of sight because of the irrepressible need they express, China's makeup and hairstyles may *look* "pinched and harassed" to an observer but they *express*, by contrast, the expansiveness and exoticism, the would-be world-travelledness of her ideal self-image—which others can only infer from the maladroit rendering on her face. In her mind's eye, China generates an inner wished-for beauty, as infinitely changeable as fantasy itself.

One further example of how the imagination supplements the power of touch, revealing its depth, occurs in *Sula*, in what is perhaps the most wholly internalized, fantastical act of beauty work Morrison has devised:

If I take a chamois and rub real hard on the bone, right on the ledge of your cheek bone, some of the black will disappear. It will flake away into the chamois and underneath will be gold leaf. I can see it shining through the black. I know it is there. . . .

And if I take a nail file or even Eva's old paring knife—that will do—and scrape away at the gold, it will fall away and there will be alabaster. . . .

Then I can take a chisel and small tap hammer and tap away at the alabaster. It will crack then like ice under the pick, and through the breaks I will see the loam, fertile, free of pebbles and twigs. . . .

I will put my hand deep into your soil, lift it, sift it with my fingers, feel its warm surface and dewy chill below. (130–31)

Mounted on her lover Ajax, determined to prolong her enjoyment of his beauty, Sula sets about undoing the work of visuality, tooling with its surfaces. The passage uncovers the dimensions that the visual has missed, allegorizing the work of attending to touch. But more than that, the passage makes literal Morrison's conception of the beauty-response as agency, something one *does*. Sula's rapturous response to her lover is so self-conscious and deliberate that it amounts to a fine craft: *"if I . . . rub . . . scrape . . . chisel . . . tap."* In her readiness and determination to get under Ajax's skin, Sula becomes carpenter, metal-smith, and farmer. Her imagination yields a whole tool-box, and together with the conceit of her lover as ebony, gold, alabaster, Sula's act of conceiving becomes beautiful too, part of the metaphor.

Sula's conceit proceeds by improvisation. It has an element of unpredictability that sets it apart from the archaic formulas of beauty that Ajax's Homeric name recalls. In Greek epic, men's beauty is described as a thin film of gold leaf that covers their flesh — something brilliant or glittering that hovers above them, covering their surface, as though beauty itself were a hard, fixed substance:

> Athena lent a hand, making him seem
> taller, and massive too, with crisping hair
> in curls like petals of wild hyacinth,
> but all red-golden. Think of gold infused
> on silver by a craftsman whose fine art
> Hephaistos taught him, or Athena; one
> whose work moves to delight: just so she lavished
> beauty over Odysseus' head and shoulders. (Homer, *The Odyssey* 105–06)

In passages such as this, the hero does not embody precious metal, as in the *blazon* tradition, but rather, receives the metal, or beauty, which is "infused on," literally "spread over" him like a helmet — the verb suggests covering or adornment, as well as the process of enameling (Cunliffe 326). Thus while the formula conveys the visual fascination, even the lingering after-image on the retina, of great beauty or renown, it also deflects attention from the hero's actual body. Morrison controverts that tradition with Sula's Ajax fantasy, suggesting that male beauty has been covered over by protective layers that need to be scrubbed off, and that the visual dimension is itself an obstacle to encountering physical beauty anew.

Beauty takes place in Morrison's novels when some act of imagination makes the body's unforeseen beauty suddenly apparent. Thus for Morrison, the experience of beauty is much more subjective and dynamic than its visual, static dimension would suggest. Beauty is ultimately improvisational, an unaccountable, unpredictable response. And beauty is narrational, for Morrison is uninterested in any notion of beauty unmediated by fantasy, storyline, the contingencies of context. Aesthetic theories ordinarily distinguish the object from the beholding of it. For example, Kant would say that Morrison's focus is not on the "beautiful *object*" per se, but rather on the "beautiful *view* of an object": "In the latter case," Kant writes, "taste appears not so much in what the imagination *apprehends*... as in the impulse it thus gets to *fiction*, i.e. in the peculiar fancies with which the mind entertains itself" (Bernard translation 81). For Kant, the beauty of an object must be distinct from the fictions it inspires, whereas for Morrison, the aesthetic object (Mavis's hands, China's face, Ajax's skin) cannot be dissociated from the montage of perceptions whereby it comes to be both felt and imagined.

Thus, in the course of Morrison's shift away from the visual and objective toward the imaginary and improvisational, there is also a radical reversal: by reminding us of the contributions of imagination to the appreciation of the body, Morrison suggests that responsiveness creates the experience of beauty, rather than the usual notion that physical beauty preexists and elicits a response. Morrison's exploration of this reverse beauty-response culminates in the prismatic portrait of Dorcas in *Jazz*, whose mysterious beauty-cum-ugliness is seen through Violet's, Alice's, Joe's, and finally Felice's eyes. For everyone but Joe, Dorcas is an assemblage of odd parts that "missed somehow." "If you looked at each thing, you would admire that thing—the hair, the color, the shape. All together it didn't fit" (201). Only Joe is able to see Dorcas whole: "the quality of her sugar-flawed skin, the high wild bush the bed pillows made of her hair, her bitten nails, the heart-breaking way she stood, toes pointed in" (28) seem ready-made to devastate him. He performs a poeisis of these fragments from the moment he sees her: "The girl buying candy and ruining her skin had moved him so his eyes burned.... the candy-counter at Duggie's where he first saw her and wondered if that, the peppermint she bought, was what insulted her skin, light and creamy everywhere but her cheeks" (29, 68).

What makes Joe's eyes burn is not so much Dorcas's physical aspect as the story he tells himself as she buys the candy—the story of a bodily marking, a mutilation, "what insulted her skin." Her peppermint-buying signals the heartbreaking lust of a little girl who underneath Jungle Red nails and grown-up stockings is another Pecola trembling to ask for Mary Janes, but the marks left by the candy, the "hooves" on her cheeks, tell a more grown-up story: of

Other Womanhood, triangulated desire, the trace of insults gone by (Alice Manfred's dreams of trampling over her rival on horseback), or insults to come (Violet's slashing at Dorcas's corpse). In portraying Joe's instantaneous, inexplicably tender response to a girl buying candy, and only later delving into Joe's history—his orphaned childhood, his childlike mother, his wife's lost daughter—Morrison illustrates what John Keats called "the innumerable compositions and decompositions which take place between the intellect and its thousand materials before it arrives at that trembling delicate and snail-horn perception of Beauty" (128). She also portrays, as Joe's obsession grows, the process that Stendhal, another witness to the unpredictability of beauty, dubbed "crystallization"—"a mental process that draws from everything that happens new proofs of the perfection of the loved one": "Even little facial blemishes...such as a smallpox scar, touch the heart of a man in love and inspire a deep reverie.... The fact is, that pockmark means a thousand things to him, mostly delightful and all extremely interesting.... Thus *ugliness* even begins to be loved and given preference, because in this case it has become beauty" (66). And yet, for Morrison, something more than Stendhal's sense of irony is at stake in ascribing beauty to bodily scars.

The treatment of disfigurements and deformities as beauty marks is tremendously important to Morrison's aesthetic, not only because Pauline's crooked ankle, Sula's birthmark, Eva Peace's missing leg, or Pilate's missing navel provoke our tactile as well as visual imagination, but because they evoke the body's touching vulnerability. Barbara Hill Rigney calls these marks of brokenness or missingness in Morrison's novels "hieroglyphs" that are "clues to a culture and a history more than to individual personality" (39). The unsightly stands in for the invisible in Morrison's aesthetic because the experience of slavery can never be recollected whole: the iron torture instruments, the traumas of the Middle Passage, that Morrison revisits only spectrally in *Beloved* necessitated their own suppression from memory. What Morrison can make vivid are the signs that are left. When Paul D runs his fingers and mouth along the trails of scar tissue on Sethe's back (17–18), there is an advent of the kind of physical beauty that interests Morrison. Paul D accesses the story of what happened to Sethe by touching her, and at the same time he beautifies her, holding in his mind's eye the image of the choke-cherry tree she suggests to him. The reader, too, can far more easily hold a tree in mind than the scene of Sethe's torture, and in this way can avoid turning away from her flayed, unforgetting back, once it is transfigured by Paul D's imagination and touch. Aside from her own story, however, Sethe's choke-cherry tree tells a more general truth about physical beauty: that the vulnerability of flesh is its true claim to beauty, that what compels our imaginations to invest the body with beauty is the feeling, literally the *pathos*, we share with others. If there is a universal recognition of physical beauty, Morrison seems to say, it has more to do with the commonality of physical suffering than with commonalities of taste, more to do with how all bodies feel rather than how they individually look:

[W]e flesh . . . Love it. Love it hard. Yonder they do not love your flesh. They despise it. They don't love your eyes; they'd just as soon pick em out. No more do they love the skin on your back. Yonder they flay it. And O my people they do not love your hands. Those they only use, tie, bind, chop off and leave empty. Love your hands! Love them. Raise them up and kiss them. Touch others with them, pat them together, stroke them on your face 'cause they don't love that either. You got to love it, you! . . . This is flesh I'm talking about here. Flesh that needs to be loved. (*Beloved* 88)

When Baby Suggs, holy, asks her congregation to touch and imagine their own beauty, she treats the body as wondrous and awe-inspiring merely because it is a thing that feels. Anatomical variables such as texture, color, or proportion could not be further from the point of this declaration of beauty. Nor does the freedom to care for the body count as the central, inviolable miracle of Baby Suggs's sermon, since slavery lies just yonder and freedom can be revoked. For Baby Suggs, the most meaningful fact about flesh is that it "needs to be loved." The body's purposiveness is not in any function it performs, but in the claim it makes on our reverence. And the only thing equal to the magnificence of the flesh's need is the imagination's power to respond: "She told them that the only grace they could have was the grace they could imagine" (*Beloved* 88). When it comes to the beauty of human bodies, Morrison suggests, the aesthetic and the political converge: physical beauty is inseparable from ethics because "it's flesh [we're] talking about here, flesh that needs to be loved."

With an awareness of how Morrison tends to devise interactions between physical touch and imagination, and how she stages beauty as a surprise effect of mental imagery brought to bear on handiwork, we can re-read the narrator's strange self-disclosure at the end of *Jazz* and understand exactly how and why the book takes a body, conveying its experience of the hands cupped around it: ". . . *I love the way you hold me, how close you let me be to you. I like your fingers on and on, lifting, turning. I have watched your face for a long time now and missed your eyes when you went away from me. . . . Look where your hands are. Now*" (229). "Lifting and turning" are words we remember from the scene of Joe and Dorcas in bed. But now that the narrator has collapsed that ill-fated affair into an idyll of Joe and Violet under the covers (on an old mattress cupped like praying hands), she collapses yet another triangle, extracting the characters from the narrator's and reader's intimacy, so that reader and narrator too are alone together between the covers of the novel, "bound and joined."

Surpassingly gorgeous, the ending of *Jazz* is a perfect example of the beauty of imagined touch, Morrison's aesthetic trademark. But it is also a remarkable feat of beauty equity, an ethical-aesthetic innovation that draws our attention to anyone's body, rather than to any one body. There is an intense apprehension of physicality at the moment of the narrator's confession; however, the intimate touch we imagine at that moment includes not only our own hands supporting the book's spine, but the hundreds of thousands of other hands that ever held a copy of *Jazz*. We are left with a great love and awe for bodies in their multiplicity, for the miracle of their common ability to feel. And this is what Morrison has always tried to portray about the beauty of physicality: that the body's aesthetic powers, that is, its feelings and perceptions, are its virtue; and that physical beauty occurs to us the moment we fully imagine the body—the moment we hold it, as we would hold a great book, in awe.

CONTENTIONS IN
THE HOUSE OF CHLOE
Morrison's Tar Baby

Maria DiBattista

Is "Once upon a time" the oldest narrative entry into the world? So con-jectures Toni Morrison in support of her belief, vigorously defended in her Nobel Laureate Address, that narrative is "one of the principal ways in which we absorb knowledge" (7). Whatever else can be inferred from such a state-ment, it is clearly *not* the remark of a born realist. Whoever resorts, as Morri-son does in her Nobel address, to fairy tale or fable to convey her attitude to-ward her craft belongs to the tribe of storytellers whose imagination may feel cramped by the form of the classic realist novel, with its absolute ban on the fabulous, mythological or miraculous. Morrison's own narratives are more hos-pitable to the presence of other-worldly creatures, to ghosts and nature spir-its, for example. Despite the fact that her books are routinely reviewed and classified as novels, one wonders, in light of the Nobel address, as august an occasion for self-definition as is likely to present itself, if Morrison even thinks of herself as primarily a novelist.

This question may strike the millions of readers who devour her books as hopelessly academic (which, of course, it is and is meant to be). Still, the popular press does not greet each new work as the newest claimant to that elusive title, the Great American Novel, but as yet another example of Mor-rison's credentials as the great American storyteller. As is often the case, the popular label gets at something fundamental about the nature of her art and

by pretending that the world is other than what it is—materially real and historically inescapable. Morrison's fiction resists making this final admission. Her art consists in always finding—or making—that "some other thing," a life and a world elsewhere, in Richard Poirier's resonant phrase. As an imaginative writer, she will not *fully* concede to the world its undislodgeable reality. She continues to dream of a belated blossoming of the real into a humanly acceptable world, even if, as in the conclusion of *The Bluest Eye*, her characters must live with the historical intuition that for them any hopes for a future flowering come "much, much, much too late" (160).

She is not alone among contemporary novelists in seeking deliverance in both fanciful and genuinely mythopoeic forms. "The anti-myths of gravity and of belonging bear the same name: flight," claims the narrator of Salman Rushdie's *Shame*, who, with a fabulist's bravura, would defy the physical laws and human bonds that tie us to the earth (86). Such defiant anti-myths emotionally exalt Morrison's protagonists as well. Her most-cherished characters are creatures of air. Flight is the dream-narrative they carry within them, inwardly buoyed, like Milkman in *Song of Solomon*, by the "sense of lightness and power" (298) the dream of flying gives them. Novelistic persons, by contrast, are weighted by gravity, grounded in the things of the earth. The burden of history is heavy upon them. Morrison's characters feel this weight, indeed often are crushed beneath it, yet they never renounce their dream of taking to the air. Their predicament preserves the antithetical meanings of flight as one of the primal words in Morrison's vocabulary: flight as a mode of transcendence most commonly associated with the imagination, especially when it takes the exalted form of prophecy; and flight as an escapist fantasy, a desperate departure from the oppressive jurisdiction of the real.

It was Harold Bloom who first took public exception to assessing Morrison's art primarily in terms of the cultural politics that ground her in time and place. He found a deeper appeal—and truth—in her representations of "the pure madness of integrities of being that cannot sustain or bear dreadful social structures." Bloom advised us to look to the "negative magic of the romancer" to account for Morrison's strengths as "a potential strong novelist." For Bloom, such strengths are not born in ideological creeds, but originate in ancestor texts: "Literary texts emerge from other literary texts and they do not choose their forerunners" ("Introduction," *Toni Morrison*, 3–4). Perhaps not. Yet in one exceptional instance Morrison not only chose a forerunner, but demanded that we read her fiction beside and against it. The title of Morrison's fourth novel, *Tar Baby*, aligns her fiction with a folkloric, primarily oral tradition, the tradition, that is, of gregarious and credulous storytellers rather than solitary and factual novelists. *Tar Baby* is in many ways Morrison's most generically mixed work and the one that, in her own interpretation, is the most obsessed with the question of masks: "The Tar Baby tale seemed to me to be about masks. Not masks as covering what is to be hidden, but how masks come to life, take life over, exercise the tensions between itself and what it covers" ("Unspeakable Things" 30). In her brief elucidation of this idea, Morrison refers primarily to the masks assumed by her characters. But it is Morrison's authorial mask of storyteller and mythographer that concerns me here and which makes me question whether Bloom, however astute in redirecting critical attention to the aesthetic character of Morrison's fiction, is altogether precise in awarding her the palm of "strong novelist." Arguably, her imaginative potencies might lie elsewhere, a proposition that cannot be confirmed until we confront the mask through which she works out her own complicated, often troubled relation to her literary heritage and unless we are willing to accept the possibility that the mask she adopts may conceal, as masks are wont to do, a divided nature.

This may strike some readers of Morrison as a misguided, even patronizing approach to a writer-critic who shows no hesitancy, much less ambivalence in identifying herself with "the dark and abiding presence" of black African-ism in American literature, a presence she insists is indisputably "there for the literary imagination as both a visible and an invisible mediating force" (*Playing* 46). Given this attestation, perhaps there is nothing at all remark-able in her having named one of her narratives after one of the most endur-ing, if also one of the most discomfiting figures in Afro-American folklore. But why select the tar baby, as mute, intractable, mesmerizing and madden-ing a black presence as any conjured up by white writing, to serve as the vis-ible emblem and mediating force for her own literary imagination? Even af-ter concluding the book, it is impossible to determine whether the title is meant to be read as eponymous or symbolic, whether it designates a charac-ter—or characters—within the book or a stereotype to be faced down and repudiated. Or is the tar baby a symbol of less determinate and even more troubling meaning, and if so, does Morrison intend to make the symbol more or less disquieting?

Transparency of meaning, much less transparency of being, is, of course, what the tar baby is designed to frustrate. The tar baby ostensibly presents an image of blackness that is infantile, impassive and inert; it embodies all the negative attributes stereotypically assigned to a certain kind of Black character — outwardly unresponsive, inactive, even sullen. Such a stereotype conforms, curiously and interestingly enough, to the way Morrison will later characterize whiteness in her influential account of how the Afro-American presence proved decisive in the shaping of American literature. In *Playing in the Dark*, Morrison, after reviewing the evidence provided by such classic American works as *Moby Dick* and *Huckleberry Finn*, concludes that "if we follow through on the self-reflexive nature of these encounters with Africanism, it falls clear: images of blackness can be evil *and* protective, rebellious *and* forgiving, fearful *and* desirable — all of the self-contradictory features of the self. Whiteness, alone, is mute, meaningless, unfathomable, pointless, frozen, veiled, curtained, dreaded, senseless, implacable" (59). All these contradictory and unfathomable, but finally artistically challenging, even irresistible attributes are manifest in what Joel Chandler Harris called "The Wonderful Story of the Tar Baby." In the tale, whatever its variations, whether, that is, it is Farmer John or Brer Fox who contrives the tar baby, the nature of the encounter is unchanged. Brer Rabbit approaches the tar baby, extends a greeting, and on receiving no response becomes increasingly exasperated. He at first slaps, then punches, then wrestles with the tar baby, each movement ensnaring him ever more securely for the predator/enemy in the wings. The non-responsiveness of the tar baby makes it initially as much an object of curiosity as of pique. Why is the greeting not returned? Is silence to be understood as a personal affront or a sign of idiocy? Or is the tale meant to illustrate a more practical lesson about the superiority of guilt to instinctive or blind aggression, especially under provocation? Or does it convey a more quietist moral — one that assumes commanding ideological force in the doctrine of non-violence — that the violence born of frustration is not only self-defeating, but indeed, self-imperilling?

Such are the questions it seems natural to put to the tale, but merely to pose them is to fall into the very trap in which Brer Rabbit, normally so clever himself, was so easily, if uncharacteristically, ensnared. The tar baby is, after all, a ruse. It is endowed with a human shape to give the impression of life where none actually exists. It presents to the onlooker who happens upon it all the arresting and unnerving features of the uncanny, at once familiar and estranged. In its apparently obstinate silence, it offends against our most civilized sense of who we are and what is due to us according to the protocols of ordinary human exchange. Its silence, which we might regard as a folkloric equivalent of Bartleby's "I prefer not to," takes us outside the bounds of sociability into some dark terrain beyond the reach of normalizing speech acts. As such, it may conveniently serve as an emblem for the written work itself, which stubbornly maintains its silence before any questions we might put to it. The title, then, not only announces a subject but issues a warning. We might read this caution as follows: reach out to this enigmatic presence that solicits you with its illusion of life; struggle to grasp this mute, inglorious image of blackness put in your path; grapple with it, chasten or reshape it, but don't expect to hold or subdue or destroy it. Or else: anything that makes blackness visible, as "un-pass-byable" as the tar baby itself, has a power, however negative or dangerous, that should not be ignored or repudiated.

Such may be the monitions that lurk in Morrison's title and dictate her literary strategies. *Tar Baby*, published in 1981, appeared after a turbulent decade when Afro-Americans were not only creating new and increasingly powerful self-images, but also contesting any depiction that did not conform to their sense of how the world appeared and felt to them. What mattered was to foreground race, not expunge or sanitize its presence in social and political representations. A decade after the publication of *Tar Baby*, Morrison was to import the racialization of American popular and political culture into the sedate preserves of the American literary canon. In *Playing in the Dark*, her influential dissection of the language of race and color in American literature, Morrison proposes that "the act of enforcing racelessness in literary discourses is itself a racial act. Pouring rhetorical acid on the fingers of a black hand may indeed destroy the prints, but not the hand. Besides, what happens in that violent, self-serving act of erasure to the hands, the fingers, the fingerprints of those who do the pouring? Do they remain acid-free? The literature itself suggests otherwise" (46). This is indeed a reasonable suggestion to draw from the literature, as long as the object of rhetorical tampering is an unnatural whiteness, a bleached-out human and social reality.

But what are the literary consequences if we reverse the terms of this proposition, as Morrison seems to have done in playing with a tar baby? What if, instead of pouring rhetorical acid on her fingers, the writer suspends them in a racial emulsion? Presumably, the signature imprint of race would then, like a photographic plate or a strip of film, yield up its hidden and hitherto invisible image. Yet there is always the attendant danger of a residue sticking to the developing hand, a residue that may constitute as telling a sign of violent and self-interested encounter as any act of erasure. The image of the manipulative hand that can destroy as well as create reappears in Morrison's Nobel Lecture, where it serves as a figure for the writer's relation to language. To illustrate her conception of the writer's vocation, Morrison retells a story, one found, she claims, in several cultures, about a wise old woman, a "rural prophet" whose fame extends beyond her community to the city, where her legend "is the source of amusement." Young skeptics, bent on exposing her as a fraud, approach her with a question they believe that, given her blindness, she will not be able to answer: "'Old woman, I hold in my hand a bird. Tell me whether it is living or dead.'" She does not answer at first, bringing her interlocutors to the brink of laughter, but at last delivers her Solomonic judgment: "'I don't know whether the bird you are holding is dead or alive, but what I do know is that it is in your hands'" (10–11).

The meaning Morrison herself chooses to read into this fable is that the bird represents language and the clairvoyant old woman the "practiced writer" embedded in a venerable, but endangered tradition. I have no quarrel with this reading, which allows Morrison to remind us of the many ways language can die: "out of carelessness, disuse, indifference, and absence of esteem, or killed by fiat" (14). Yet what detains me is the distinction hovering at the edges of her fable between what we might call the writer's custodial hand, which cherishes and protects the cultural lore entrusted to its keeping, and the manipulative hand that, concerned only with asserting its own power, suffocates the living language within its deadly grasp. Interpreted in light of this recurrent imagery of manipulation, the tar baby suddenly reveals itself as a race-specific emblem for the black artist's ambiguous relation to black matter — black culture, black history and black story, especially the unspeakable and unspoken story that will not be told until *Beloved*, a story that possibly could not be told until Morrison herself had survived her own encounter with the tar baby put in her path.

In assessing the validity of reading *Tar Baby* as a cautionary tale about the risks inherent in black writing, subjective and objective genitive, we might consider Morrison's own interpretation of the tale. "It was," she remembers thinking, "a rather complicated story with a funny happy ending about the triumph of cunning over law, of wit over authority, of weakness over power." This reading, while granting the story's complicated morality, immediately disposes of any troublesome after-thoughts about the "funny happy ending" by supplying the appropriate moral: the story celebrates the triumph of cunning over law, wit over authority, weakness over power. This is a plausible, if somewhat tidy account of how the denouement works on our moral sensibility, yet it fails signally to satisfy the one person most invested in it—Morrison herself. As she later confides, the story continued to worry her, a worry linked to the uncanniness of the aesthetic object: "Why did the extraordinary solution the farmer came up with to trap the rabbit involve tar? Why was the rabbit's sole area of vulnerability having good manners? Why did the tar baby's silent complicity seem to me at once natural and obscene? Of the two views of the Brier Patch, the farmer's and the rabbit's, which was right? Why did it all seem so contemporary and, more to the point, so foreboding?" (quoted in O'Meally, "Tar Baby" 36). In eliciting the contemporary resonance of the tale, Morrison knew she would be resuscitating its foreboding elements as well. These forebodings appear to be connected to her sense of the way the story questions the moral good of good manners, rendering it vulnerable to an impolite silence that is at once natural and obscene. Yet why should an act of discourtesy inspire such hysterical reaction on the part of the rabbit and such writerly distress, amounting to a dark foreboding, in Morrison? There hardly seems to be much matter for unnerving concern, unless we take into account Morrison's own relation to the story.

Morrison figures this relation in a gesture that falls far beneath Brer's Rabbit's impatient, chastising cuff. "I did not retell that story," Morrison confided. "And needless to say, I did not improve it. I fondled it, scratched and pressed it with my fingertips as one does the head and spine of a favorite cat—to get at the secret of its structure without disturbing its mystery" (quoted in O'Meally, "Tar Baby," 36). Here the writerly hand is not depicted pouring acid on its materials, but gently pressuring its valued object to surrender its secret. Importantly, the secret of the tale must be coaxed rather than dragged forth to ensure that its core mystery is left intact. The enigma of the tale must be deciphered, but not demystified, a rather neat, but, for Morrison, an essential distinction. With such hermeneutic dexterity, Milkman decodes the children's playground song in which is encrypted the story of his ancestry, without disturbing its power to enchant. Such reverence for occult realities dictates Morrison's approach to the mythological and folkloric material. Her narratives appeal to the numinous registers of fable for enlightenment, for a salivific meaning not to be found in the demythologized world of everyday life, the world, that is, represented most scrupulously by the novel. Rather than strike at an elusive, even offending mystery (as Ahab contemplated striking the sun if it dared insult him) into forced counter-response, Morrison strokes and caresses it. What she does not do is address it from a safe distance. Contact, with all the risk of entanglement, even soilage that might entail, is the only envisioned course. But why take these risks or hazard such contaminations?

The opening sentence of *Tar Baby*—"He believed he was safe"—suggests one possible motive. Morrison may simply feel that safety in any case is impossible and, as we shall see, ignoble to boot. In her own commentary on the beginning of this work, she relates how she carefully set the verb "believed" within an anapestic rhythm to produce the desired, but deceptive effect of existential as well as metric stability. "If I had wanted the reader to trust this person's point of view," she writes, "I would have written 'was safe.' Or, 'Finally, he was safe.' The unease about this view of safety is important because safety itself is the desire of each person in the novel. Locating it, creating, it losing" ("Unspeakable Things" 30). To this inventory of those made uneasy by the prospect of locating, creating or losing safety we must add Morrison herself.

This, too, the opening pages of the narrative make clear in a near-paroxysm of narrative unease. The book commences with a nameless figure plunging into the sea believing that he can master its currents, gain the shore, and with it, his freedom. But it is no ordinary sea to which he commits himself. Everywhere there are symbolic signs that a romancer, not a naturalist, is imagining a world for him to navigate. Even the signatories of the made human world are imbued with a romantic luster: the ship from which he dives bears the regal name Konigsgaarten, the king of the seas, and the port town that awaits its docking is Queen of France. It is the first image of potential, perhaps predestined mating in a book whose last, hallucinatory image of coupling is the marriage flight of a queen soldier ant and her chosen consort, "the man who fucked like a star" (292). Novelistic descriptions of human lovemaking, even of the most passionate order, cannot hope to compete with such stellar instances of sexual transport. Contributing to the exciting sense of romantic ordeal is the swimmer's encounter with the "water-lady" whose insistent hand "was forcing him away from the shore": "[she] cupped him in the palm of her hand, and nudged him out to sea" (5). Morrison again figures authorial power—here her own power as a "negative romancer"—in the image of the intruding and intervening hand. In this instance, however, the fateful hand is acting upon and within a primordial environment in which race is not yet an issue. Blackness is the color of the sea or of the night sky, a temporary if spectacular coloration, not an indelible racial marker. The water-lady and her sheltering, but insistent hand is the narrative delegate for Morrison's own romance proclivities. In and through her, she enjoys trying her own writerly hand at recounting one of those thrilling sea-adventures that, since the days of Odysseus, challenge the storyteller, schooled in tradition, to exercise his ingenuity. Yet generically as well as episodically speaking, the swimmer's safety is never seriously threatened by the hand of a water-lady or the female romancer she might personify as author. The only real peril he encounters takes the form of an impersonal natural force. Caught in its grip, the swimmer is "down, down and found himself not at the bottom of the sea, as he expected, but whirling in a vortex. He thought nothing except, I am going counterclockwise. No sooner had he completed the thought than the sea flattened and he was riding its top" (4).

Riding can take on the dimensions of mythological feat in Morrison's fiction—one remembers the eerie last line of *Song of Solomon* celebrating the shamanistic knowledge that inspires Milkman's suicidal leap: "If you surrendered to the air, you could *ride* it" (337). Surviving the downward thrust of the whirlpool thus delivers the fugitive not only from a treacherous natural phenomenon but from a literary hazard—the vortex of realism, we might call it. Milkman refuses to be engulfed by it, demonstrating an imaginative as well as physical courage that Morrison, his creator, apparently affirms. This aspect of her narrative desire to defy the tenets, indeed the physical laws which realism is bound to honor, is epitomized in the figure of the water-lady, who presumably desires to prevent the swimmer from reaching shore. Once grounded in the verisimilar world, he might find safety, but *her* existence would be imperilled, deprecated as the insubstantial stuff of fable. The water-lady wants to detain him "at sea," captive to the world of romance. The vortex which competes for his life is an antagonist force that cannot be so fancifully personified. Its eddies are formed by commingling currents of physical facts; at their center is a vacuum in which fantasy and dream may find room to circulate, but no safe, permanent quarter. This the nameless fugitive subliminally apprehends. What saves him from such an engulfing physical realism is not a supernatural agent, but a reflex of his own observing consciousness. Completing the thought—or, to be accurate, impersonally remarking his own movement—seems to work as a counter-charm to the spiraling downward motion. This moment of self-objectification *rhetorically* delivers him to the surface, where he will eventually make his way to a shore which at first he cannot see, which is just as well, advises the narrator, fond of both legend and irony, "because he was gazing at the shore of an island that, three hundred years ago, had stuck slaves blind the moment they saw it" (8).

The race descended from these slaves still roams the island, which bears the name, Isle of Chevaliers, after their own uncanny power of riding "through the rain forest avoiding all sorts of trees and things" (152–53). Such is the "fisherman's tale" that is later recounted to the fugitive about the legendary race of blind horsemen who will call out to him in the last pages of the book. His informant also tells him that "Personally I think the blindness comes from second-degree syphilis" (153). But in Morrison's fiction, science is generally ineffectual in challenging the knowledge—and solace—offered by fable. "Realistic" explanations of the world do not deter her imaginative (hence most beloved) characters from taking flight into the dream territories that shimmer, like a mirage, beyond the horizons of the Real. The book will end with the fugitive running "Lickety split. Lickety-split. Lickety-lickety-lickety-split" to join those blind chevaliers who "race those horses like angels all over the hills" (306). In rhythmic homage to Brer Rabbit's high-tailing it out of danger, Morrison elects to return her fiction to the idiom as well as the realm of folktale. A book that begins with an empowering, if morally questionable belief in safety thus concludes with a final scramble into myth and the legendary community one might find there. Morrison has commented on this symmetry in a manner that interests us. The close of the book, she points out, entails the "wide and marvelous space between the contradiction of those two images: from a dream of safety to the sound of running feet. The whole mediated world in between" ("Unspeakable Things" 31).

The "whole mediated world in between" I take to refer to the province of the novel and it is clear by the ending of this, as of many of her works, that Morrison is not ready to settle down there. The novel for her is a space for imaginative transit, never a final destination. The prosaic world does not inspire her deepest loyalty, although it necessarily commands her respect and quite often her most hilarious as well as most heart-breaking satire. As a novel about the prosaic world, Tar Baby can only be said to begin at the point numerically and typographically marked with a 1, consigning the previous narrative to prologue or antechamber to the main structure of the narrative. The opening sentence of this new chapter confirms the necessity for imaginative re-orientation: "The end of the world, as it turned out, was nothing more than a collection of magnificent winter houses on Isle des Chevaliers" (9).

Nothing is more efficient in Morrison's rhetorical arsenal for demolishing the empire of fancy than the corrective force of that knowing, almost patronizing phrase — "as it turned out." It summarily chastises any extravagant imaginings with the incontrovertible evidence of facts — like names and places that have a specific provenance in time. But it also must be said that there is a fine disdain for the wealth of material facts the novel may offer in the way the narrator dismisses a collection of magnificent winter homes as a mere "nothing" compared to the wonderlands fancy can conjure.

The characters who inhabit these novelistic environs are neither the archetypal adventurers of romance, nor the dispossessed sons or mistreated daughters of fable and fairy tale. They are the settled members of a household presided over by Valerian Street, heir to a candy fortune who has retired to the Isle de Chevaliers. They live in a " 'handsomely articulated and blessedly unrhetorical house'" (11) whose name, L'Arbre de la Croix, suggests that Valerian's refuge will soon, if it has not already, become his Golgotha. In this house are congregated the principal players of Morrison's interracial drama: Valerian the patriarch, his wife Margaret, the former beauty queen (or Principal Beauty as she is sarcastically called), their black servants Sydney and Ondine, "Philadelphia Negroes" of correct deportment, and their niece Jade, whose education Valerian has sponsored. There is also a resident "ghost" in the family ensemble, the Street's son Michael. Around him Morrison accumulates all the novelistic lore of social activism that links *Tar Baby* to a certain historical era — to the days of Dick Gregory for President, of agitation for Indian rights and the return to a barter rather than free market economy.

It is into this household that the fugitive intrudes, bearing with him all the explosive power of romance. Morrison arranges for him a somewhat comical, if suspenseful entry. Margaret, determined to resolve a dispute with her husband, goes to her room to look for a poem, but instead discovers a black man hiding in her closet. Sydney, with the aid of .32 caliber pistol, escorts him to the dining room where the family is assembled, while Ondine volunteers to call the Harbor police. Everyone reacts with proper alarm, except Valerian, who cordially greets his "guest" and asks him if he cares to have a drink. Valerian's welcoming gesture catapults us into a novel of Faulknerian outrage. The women are outraged at the offense to their womanhood (which has been affrighted); Sydney and Ondine, who have never been invited to share the table with Valerian and Margaret, are outraged at the discourtesy to themselves. Later Valerian will compound the offense to domestic propriety by christening the fugitive-intruder Son, a name that signifies his symbolic rather than biological place in Valerian's affections.

Only belatedly do we come to know that the black man has a name, William Green, and that he comes equipped with a decidedly "novelistic" history—childhood memories, a broken marriage, a nomadic life as an "undocumented man" in "an international legion of day laborers and musclemen, gamblers, sidewalk merchants, migrants, unlicensed crewmen on ships with volatile cargo, part-time mercenaries, full-time gigolos, or curbside musicians" (166). Had Morrison made *this* derelict life the center of her novel, Green might well have found himself the protagonist of a naturalist novel in the Dreiserian mode. But she made a Caribbean Isle, not the grimy back-streets of port towns or the crowded alleyways of third-world bazaars the setting of her story. It is in a landscape hospitable to myth that she confers this novelistic identity upon him, as if to see if it will survive there or revert to some other, more primordial state of being. We can gauge his progress—or regress, as the case may be—simply by noting the names that define him at any given time in the narrative, whose human relations are coded, as it were, by the presence or absence of color. Morrison enjoys scrambling colors in her racial palette, especially in this novel where red, white, green, yellow, and of course black stand as primary signatures of character as well as indices of social status. Naming her lovers Green and Jade, for example, hints at a complementariness that sexually draws them to each other despite the vast difference in class, education, and experience separating them.

The courtship of Jade and Son will proceed in counterpoint to the emotional disintegration of the House of Valerian. Two narrative tracks are thus laid, as it were, side by side, sometimes crossing and bisecting each other, but bound for separate narrative destinations. Let us consider first the "novelistic" trajectory. By the books's novelistic but not literal end, the moral compromises and self-flattering, exculpatory fictions that have kept the Valerian household emotionally solvent are liquidated in a veritable orgy of truth-telling. This family plot is thus put in the service of the reality principle. It seeks out social and personal truth in its most unpalatable, but also most undeniable form. To do this it must vanquish the human disposition to replace unbearable reality with fantasy- anodynes, a disposition symbolized by Valerian's name, whose family name, Street, comments ironically on any personal fancies he might entertain to disguise the truth of his life. Street is a rather common thoroughfare—as compared, say, to the more aristocratic boulevard or avenue. Valerian bespeaks of aristocratic, even imperial pretensions, and indeed Valerian prides himself in being named after a Roman Emperor. But the name Valerian also possesses a more ambiguous, even sinister significance. Valerian is a plant form with spiky flowers from whose roots is derived a sedative and anti-spasmodic. Sedation appears to be one of its "true and ancient properties," to invoke the standard Morrison adopts in dedicating the novel to her female progenitors and relations.

This dedication is worth pausing over, since within it is secreted the moral by which the fiction and its characters will be called to account: "Mrs. Caroline Smith, Mrs. Millie McTyeire, Mrs. Ardelia Willis, Mrs. Ramah Wofford, and Mrs. Lois Brooks—and each of their sisters, all of whom knew their true and ancient properties." Unlike *Song of Solomon,* which bears the singular and intimate dedication, Daddy, *Tar Baby* pays homage to an entire line of female forbears. How uncompromisingly historical is that catalogue of names, particularly striking given Morrison's belief in the demiurgic power of names. These names are culled from the unremarkable ledgers of daily life. You might find such names in a phone book, where I suspect, some of them might still be found. What distinguishes these women is not the symbolic import of their names, but the knowledge they possess and preserve in the form of "ancient properties." This collective inheritance is at once evoked and jeopardized by the epigraph that succeeds and complements the dedication, take from First Corinthians 1:11: "For it hath been declared unto me of you, my brethren by them which are of the house of Chloe, that there are contentions among you." Paul's admonition carries with it an entreaty to end division, and a way of attaining that end: "Now I beseech you, brethren, by the name of our Lord Jesus Christ, that ye all speak the same thing; and that there be no divisions among you; but that ye be perfectly joined together in the same mind and in the same judgment." Paul, voicing a millenarian ideal of spiritual accord, summons us to a heavenly community in which we all will be of the same mind, share the same judgment and so speak the same things. But the novel is a dialogic form that gives expression to different minds and utters diverse judgements on the things of this world. The novel's generic obligation to render unto Caesar everything that is Caesar's, to render, that is, the material and historical world with impartiality, may explain why Morrison, for whom First Corinthians is a formative "precursor" text, regards the novelistic inheritance as spiritually inadequate to her needs. No matter how bleak the story she has to tell, the history she must relate, she never loses faith in this Pauline vision of a spirit and a community perfected through love.

But if the dedication and epigraph announces the spiritual disposition of the narrative that follows, it also declares a personal lineage. The author who now bears the name of Toni Morrison was born Chloe Anthony Wofford, a name she changed to Toni during her years at Howard, and to Morrison in 1958 upon her marriage. Reading *back* into the dedication through the epigraph, we see Morrison reclaiming her ancestral house, publicly honoring the female clan from which she descends and whose enduring, formal existence we might recognize under the name of the House of Chloe. This is the only instance I know of in Morrison's writings where her given name is read as a prophetic signature in the Joycean mode, reconnecting her, as Stephen Dedalus's name links him to the artificers of old, to her true and ancient properties. Among these we must reckon the true and ancient properties of storytelling.

Tar Baby, like many of Morrison's fictions, is filled with storytellers who act as her surrogates. They devise or invent stories in order to make sense of the world; for them narrative truly functions, as Morrison puts it in her Nobel Address, as a form of knowledge. But the sense they make may not always *make* sense. Narrative may be a way of knowing, but making up stories can as easily occlude as disclose the truth about things. "You making up a life that nobody is living," Sydney reprimands Ondine when she begins to tell her version of why Michael will never return, as his mother expects, for Christmas (36). Or sometimes the sheer inventiveness of the storyteller can exhaust the resources of a language, and hence obliterate any way of determining what is fact, what invention, what an outright falsehood. Thus Thérèse, a blind, shamanistic old woman not unlike the one Morrison celebrates in her Laureate address, fabricates a story about Son and Jade rooted in the belief that Son is a horseman descended from the hills, a story whose every detail departs further and further from the truth: "The more she invented the more she rocked and the more she rocked the more her English crumbled till finally it became dust in her mouth stopping the flow of her imagination and she spat it out altogether and let the story shimmer through the clear cascade of the French of Dominique" (108). Untranslated and perhaps untranslatable, Thérèse's story can convince and instruct no-one. Its shimmering form fails to grasp or arrest an image of truth: whatever wisdom she possesses is drowned in the cascade of her invention, which dazzles but does not enlighten.

Morrison's own instincts about how best to tell a story and coax forth the secret of its structure represent a modification and refinement of the survival instinct manifest in the fugitive's talent for fashioning a story to suit his audience: "The sex, weight and demeanor of whomever he encountered would inform and determine his tale" (5). Morrison pays tribute here to storytelling as an invaluable human resource for the defenseless or disadvantaged — tales can function as survival narratives, securing our safety by enlisting the listener on our behalf. The personal proximity the storyteller enjoys, the proximity that skill can turn into valuable intimacy, is unavailable to the novelist. Moreover, the tale the novelist has to tell is embedded in a reality that may not be so easily altered to suit the audience and occasions of its telling. For there is another instinct at work in the novelist even more powerful than the instinct to survive, an instinct whose vicissitudes deeply concern Morrison. She alludes to it in a particularly stark moment in the narrative when Valerian Street finally is told the reason why, in his childhood, his son Michael had hidden under the sink: "The instinct of kings was always to slay the messenger, and they were right. A real messenger, a worthy one, is corrupted by the message he brings. And if he is noble he should accept that corruption" (243).

This remark falls under the convention of authorial commentary, but in this instance the observation seems to refer less to the events within the narrative than to the author's attitude toward her material and her mission as a truth-teller. This may be why this thought is expressed as a maxim, a proverbial truth not so much about the historical fate of royal messengers as the likely fate awaiting that truth-teller, the novelist. It is as a novelist, not as a storyteller, that Morrison recounts the corrupting message that Valerian does not want to hear — how his young wife, despite her protestations that "I am not one of those women in the *National Enquirer*," abused their young son ("you stuck pins in his behind. You burned him with cigarettes") (209). That the *National Enquirer* might be seen as a rival, or at least a consumer, of the *kinds* of horror that Morrison recounts suggests how extensive the perceived threat of "corruption" can be. The family history of child abuse in the Valerian household and the sensational story of how Son accidentally murdered his wife, caught in a liaison with a teenage boy, are fodder for tabloid mentalities. Morrison writes in the tradition of Faulknerian outrage, understanding, as Faulkner did, how uncomfortably and often comically close are the tales and the rhetoric of the sensationalist press and their chosen style of novelistic reportage. It is a style adapted to the conditions of life in the Gothic and grotesque landscapes of dream and dementia, the style of history's losers and victims. For Morrison, as I have argued, this understanding of possible contagion is figured in the image of the authorial hand immersing itself in such "dark" material that it may itself become stained, hopelessly entangled in the evil it reports. Being a messenger, then, means being corrupted by the message that no-one wants to hear.

Morrison displays her fearlessness, some might say her disregard for credibility, in dramatizing her divided artistic allegiances in a scene which involves both an allegorical and real encounter with tar. Jade, the most "novelistic," cosmopolitan character in the novel, at home in Paris and New York and having no relation to Nature except as a pleasure ground, wanders off the road where her car has stalled and suddenly finds herself in a bog, up to her knees in tar. Jade, who will later be called a "tar baby" by Son, is here experiencing the panic of a female Brer Rabbit. What assails her is not the materiality of tar, but the reality of blackness that her own light-colored skin has allowed her to avoid. We first come to know Jade "psychologically" through a recurrent dream. In the dream she relives an uncanny moment in a Paris supermarket when a splendid black woman with skin the color of tar, carrying three eggs, catches Jade in her gaze and then directs a stream of spit at her feet. The egg-bearing "woman's woman—that mother/sister/she" (46)—transports Jade to some primordial realm of femaleness located "at the edge of the world."

Son, too, thought he had glimpsed some dreamscape at the "end of the world" where he might make a home. But unlike him, Jade is not a creature responsive to the lure of supermundane beings and their apocalyptic ultimates. She is a "character" in a novel who finds the very idea of such a woman and such a world repugnant, if mesmerizing. She is continually haunted by spectral women fingering eggs and baring their milk-giving breasts, but none will be as insistent as the forest-women who regard her, at first desirously, then reproachfully, as she struggles to liberate herself from tar:

The young tree sighed and swayed. The women looked down from the rafters of the trees and stopped murmuring. They were delighted when they first saw her, thinking a runaway child had been restored to them. But upon looking closer they saw differently. This girl was fighting to get away from them. The women hanging from the trees were quiet now, but arrogant—mindful as they were of their value, their exceptional femaleness; knowing as they did that the first world of the world had been built with their sacred properties; that they alone could hold together the stones of the pyramids and the rushes of Moses's crib; knowing their steady consistency, their pace of glaciers, their permanent embrace, they wondered at the girl's desperate struggle down below to be free, to be other than they were. (183)

Jade, schooled to live in the metropolitan world, takes flight *from* this elemental, antediluvian first world of the world, this world of exceptional femaleness, all breasts and eggs. There is something grotesquely comic in Morrison's flagrant sexual symbolism here, which makes us sympathize with Jade's disgust with the local culture of female necromancy (a culture that shares the dark humor that often infuses folktale, like naming a swamp *Sein de Vieilles*). What detains us in this gynocratic phantasmagoria is the talismanic phrase "sacred properties," which emotionally reconnects us to the women cited in the book's dedication. We cannot dismiss the implication that Morrison herself is the legatee destined to receive and in her turn transmit custodianship of those ancient properties, the well-spring of the first stories told of the world, from the saga of pyramids built by slaves to the divine story of Moses found in the bulrushes.

For Morrison these properties signify and ensure the endurance of tradition—consistency, change that is non-convulsive, but deeply considered and steadily pursued. Of these, the most important as well as most difficult for Morrison to remember is the *glacial pace* by which human life and human culture should be advanced. Temperamentally, she is kin to Thérèse and prefers a cascade of invention to the glacial and stately tread mandated by tradition. She is more likely to break into a narrative run, lickety-split, lickety-split, than retard the momentum of the stories that are spilling out of her brain. Two kinds of exceptional femaleness are brought together in this passage, and in their encounter we might detect the figure of Morrison the storyteller, imaginatively at home in the elemental world of myth, confronting Morrison the truth-teller, who must, like Jade, make her living, even if it corrupts her, in the mediated world.

In *Tar Baby* the contention between these two narrative selves is never completely resolved. Perhaps this is the why the narrative concludes not with a celebration of female properties, but with the cheering on of a "certain kind of man," in the hope, perhaps, that he will find a way out of the impasse in which Morrison has landed him. This is how Morrison understands him:

He was dwelling on his solitude, rocking the wind, adrift. A man without human rites: unbaptized, uncircumcised, minus puberty rites or the formal rites of manhood. Unmarried and undivorced. He attended no funeral, married in no church, raised no child. Propertyless, homeless, sought for but not after. There were no grades given in his school, so how could he know when he had passed? He used to want to go down in blue water, down, down, then to rise and burst from the waves to see before him a single hard surface, a heavy thing, but intricate. He would enclose it, conquer it, for he knew his power then. And it was perhaps because the world knew it too that it did not consider him able. The conflict between knowing his power and the world's opinion of it secluded him, made him unilateral. But he had chosen solitude and the company of other solitary people — opted for it when everybody else had long ago surrendered, because he never wanted to live in the world their way. There was something wrong with the rites. He had wanted another way. Some other way of being in the world.... (165–66)

Such a man may rightly expect to be welcomed among the blind chevaliers who live beyond the reach of any human laws, customs or rites. It is, I suppose, one way of being in the world and one way of defying, like Milkman, the unbearable gravity of being.

But it is not the way of being in the world of the novel, which encompasses multilateral, not singular humanity. Morrison is drawn to such unilateral beings, those isolatoes that populate American romances, who carry within them the seeds of some primordial maleness, the generative power celebrated in *Song of Solomon*. But the exhilaration in recovering a lost patrimony that exalts that fiction at its end becomes muted in her succeeding work. *Tar Baby*, indeed, occupies a problematic place in Morrison's career, interposing between the patriarchal exaltation of *Song of Solomon* and the maternal pathos of *Beloved*. At its conclusion, its lovers are in flight, Jade taking to the air, Son to the hills. We gather, then, that contentions still persist in the House of Chloe. Yet with this knowledge comes a compensatory vision, a vision granted us at a certain point in the narrative, a point of rest and contemplation in which Morrison instructs as follows:

At some point in life the world's beauty becomes enough. You don't need to photograph, paint or even remember it. It is enough. No record of it needs to be kept and you don't need someone to share it with or tell it to. When that happens —

that letting go — you let go because you can. The world will always be there — while you sleep it will be there — when you wake it will be there as well. So you can sleep and there is reason to wake. A dead hydrangea is as *intricate* and lovely as one in bloom. Bleak sky is as seductive as sunshine, miniature orange trees without blossom or fruit are not defective; they are that. (242, emphasis added)

This is the only purely aesthetic sentiment expressed in *Tar Baby*, and certainly the most serene expression of Morrison's lyricism. It surfaces unexpectedly, like a sudden infusion of grace, in the midst of a series of moral reckonings: Margaret, the monster-mother begging Ondine for forgiveness and friendship; Valerian indicting himself for the "crime of innocence" that makes him "inhuman and therefore unworthy" (241, 243). The oddity of this moment cannot be minimized. The things of this world are perceived for what they are rather than for what they might signify and what they are, it turns out, is beautiful. Beautiful and *intricate* . . . one last time, at least in this essay, we encounter a trope of entanglement and perplexity. The world will always be there to enchant and ensnare us — this is the humbling truth subtending Morrison's storytelling art — and its strange consolation.

Strange, because such a vision seems hardly supportable, given the history of the world, and indeed for Morrison, most often it is not. Morrison, of course, has shown herself in her writing to be uncommonly sensitive to the sheer gorgeousness of the language of pain and contention, as reported in the House of Chloe. But she is equally haunted by the Pauline judgment that the world is subject to perpetual indictment for the very qualities — loveliness and intricacy — that appeal to the artist in her. Another storyteller-novelist tormented by similar self-divisions, Salman Rushdie, poses the same quandary in *The Moor's Last Sigh*. "How to forgive the world for its beauty," a Mephistopholean-inquisitor demands to know at the close of the Moor's long journey into art, "which merely disguises its ugliness; for its gentleness, which merely cloaks its cruelty; for its illusion of continuing, seamlessly, as the night follows the day, so to speak — whereas in reality life is a series of brutal ruptures, falling upon our defenseless heads like the blows of a woodsman's axe?" (391). How indeed? Rhetorically as substantially, the argument remains unsettled. But the arraignment of the world as a place of insidious beauty and treacherous illusion could not have been so forcefully, so vividly made without Rushdie's final simile of the woodsman's axe. It is to fable and fairy tale that we must look to understand, indeed to bear, the mortal blows that life rains upon us.

So we conclude, then, as we begun, by meditating on the kind of knowledge to be found in fable, where the woodsman's axe still falls with deadly authority. We know that there will be contentions among us — the House of Chloe issues bulletins to that effect. We suspect to the point of certainty that the romancer in Morrison, always poised for flight, and the novelist in her, mired in the corruptions of truth, will continue to struggle for mastery over the Real. Yet for readers of Morrison, incapable, as Morrison's imaginary creatures are, of taking flight lickety-split into folktale and myth, there is comfort in knowing that the world is not cursed, only intricate. Certainly Morrison appears to find solace in reaching that point in her art when she can let go, relax her grip and admit, without bitterness, that the world will always be there. In such moments of respite and reprieve, when the world is apprehended as merely but *fully* there, its beauty sufficient to our needs, the romancer and the novelist in Morrison, seem, however impermanently, reconciled. The denunciatory force of Morrison's social representations are not so much opposed, but consumed in such moments of harmony. These are the times of concord in the House of Chloe, when all, if only for a brief while, are of the same mind and judgment.

Sensations of Loss

Michael Wood

"The language of a novel is the system of its 'languages.'"
M. M. Bakhtin, *The Dialogic Imagination*

One of the most striking features of Toni Morrison's fiction is the brilliance of its apparently casual, often bleak insights; what it knows without seeming to know at all. "The neighbors seemed pleased when the babies smothered.... They did all the right things, of course: brought food, telephoned their sorrow, got up a collection; but the shine of excitement in their eyes was clear" (*Paradise* 21). The reporter who interviews the mother of the smothered babies is sympathetic, her eyes are "soft"; "but the shine was like that of the neighbors" (22).

Sometimes, especially in the earlier novels, these insights are discreetly highlighted as authorial knowledge, and in *Jazz* they are given to an identifiable female narrator, who is always shrewd and entertaining but sometimes wrong. Most often, though, the insights are closely aligned with particular characters. In these cases there is no authorial knowledge, we might say, or there are several knowledges. The author knows only what her characters know, and they know different, contradictory things. The narrative voice is steady, ample, eloquent, recognizably Morrison's own; but what it says comes from marked places within the fiction, articulating what is seen along quite different lines of sight. This effect is allowed its furthest, most difficult development in *Paradise*, and an understanding of how it works there will teach us a good deal about the density of the novel's argument about race, the complexity of its meditation on history, and the deep ambiguities generated by the dead and living bodies of its multiple conclusions. My suggestion is that in *Paradise* Morrison not only re-enacts, by example, the questions raised by the emergence of competing knowledges, but also refigures knowledge itself in the light of what fiction can and cannot do; construes knowledge as a dialogue between canceled and continuing possibilities.

Who knows about the neighbors' and the reporter's excitement about the smothered babies, for example? Who sees the shine in their eyes, to whose perception do they "seem" pleased? An omniscient narrator would not need to report appearances in this way, and the mother of the dead children is too bewildered and distraught to reach for these interpretations. Too inarticulate to formulate them at any time, perhaps, but the feelings can only be hers, she is guiding us here. She is doing the seeing, even if she is not conscious of it; Morrison has lent her the shape and lucidity of the sentences. This is not an unusual or original technique—it is much used in Flaubert, Faulkner, Woolf, Henry James, and García Márquez—but I think its reach and its delicacy have been underestimated. We seem to be much more comfortable with intense and plausible impersonations of character or a declared ironic distance from them. We are also more comfortable with various versions of *style indirect libre*, where the author/narrator ironically, unobtrusively borrows the tone and language of a character. Morrison uses this method too, but it is at its most interesting when it starts to slide back toward the other one.

"God at their side, the men take aim" (18). These men are murdering women the way earlier generations burned witches, and for similar reasons, so the narrator cannot be telling us they really had God at their side. If the men are likely to have said to themselves that God is at their side—and some of them are—then this is a moment of *style indirect libre*. If the men are likely to have felt a mixture of excitement and fear and outraged virtue, but to have lacked an image with which to represent and cancel these feelings—as most of them probably did—we are back with a narrator who finds language for feelings which are not hers, but which are there in the fiction, waiting to be named. There are nine men involved, so it is appropriate for a range of meanings to lurk in the single simple phrase.

Commentators tend to agree about the attributes of Morrison's style, even when they disagree about whether they like it or not. When Jill Mathus writes of a "rich and startling lyricism" (156), and Henry Louis Gates and Anthony

Appiah evoke "a densely lyrical narrative texture that is instantly recognizable" (xi), they are being complimentary about what James Wood sees as a problem of purple prose (236–45). Phrases taken in isolation may incline us to Wood's view, but the issue of taste is immediately complicated by other issues, and I want to look at the question from the reverse side: not how Morrison speaks for her characters but how they speak through her and if they speak through her. What happens when the lyricism, like the knowledge, is theirs rather than hers? And when it is not?

Mile after mile rolled by urged and eased by the gorgeous ache in Bennie's voice. (35)

Somewhere in the house the child continued to cry, filling Sweetie with rapture — she had never heard that sound from her own. Never heard that clear yearning call, sustained, rhythmic. It was like an anthem, a lullaby, or the bracing chords of the decalogue. (129–30)

The wind soughed as though trying to dislodge sequins from the black crepe sky. Lilac bushes swished the side of the house. (190)

She entered the vice like a censored poet whose suspect lexicon was too supple, too shocking to punish. (261)

September marched through smearing everything with oil paint: acres of caradamom yellow, burnt orange, miles of sienna, blue ravines both cerulean and midnight, along with heartbreakingly violet skies. (232)

These five quotations picture the worlds and feelings and activities of five different women. The first is Mavis, the mother of the smothered children, who has run away from the rest of her family and is on the road, driving west. Bennie is a hitchhiker who sings all the time: "Songs of true love, false love, redemption; songs of unreasonable joy. . . . Mavis sang along once in a while, but mostly she listened . . ." (34). The "gorgeous ache" is not what Bennie's voice possesses, or not necessarily. It is what Mavis hears in it, what Mavis misses when Bennie is gone. More precisely, it is what Mavis would call it if she had such words. It is a name for what she cannot name, the sound of an experience turning into a regret, an absence. Of course there may be an ache behind the ache in Bennie's voice, the force of Bennie's own real pain, but the adjective "gorgeous" pulls us emphatically away from that.

The second woman is Sweetie, mother of four extremely sick children, who seem never to have had a moment's health. Her own mind is stretched to the breaking point by weariness and worry, and she has walked away from her house into the wind and snow. She sees the girl who tries to help her as a personification of Sin, and the women who take her in as hawks and demons. The child she hears crying is either a product of her own imagination — released from sickness into temporary madness she hears the sound of health — or one of Mavis's dead children, who have been haunting the house since Mavis arrived. Either way the yearning is Sweetie's, rather than that of the child, and the images offered to us — anthem, lullaby, decalogue — all come from her emotional world, if not from her vocabulary.

The third woman is Patricia, schoolteacher and amateur historian. Troubled by all she knows and suspects, she opens her window and looks out across the yard towards her mother's grave. The soughing wind and the sequins are her metaphors — slightly old-fashioned, a literary consolation which cannot quite console, as if Patricia had quoted a poem which does not cheer her up as much as she thought it would.

The fourth woman is Seneca, the girl who seeks to help Sweetie, and who finds her own consolation and distraction in cutting herself repeatedly, obsessively. Here the simile — even the word "vice" — cannot be hers, and seems so far removed from anything she can be feeling that we have to suspect the intervention of the novelist herself, or one of her literary surrogates. The writer sees the girl's thrill at the self-scarring, but must translate it, for herself and for us, into something less secret, more negotiable. "Too shocking" looks like a cover for something which is beyond or beneath shock.

The fifth quotation evokes the landscape of a brief and beautiful love affair. The oil paint and its colors are a metaphor for the riotous change in the life of Connie, who has fallen in love with a man for the first time at the age of thirty-nine. Nothing in the language or the perception belongs to her — nothing except the tumult and the brightness, that is. Paint here plays something of the role of literature in the previous example: it talks to us about the character, but not from within the character's mind.

What do these instances show us? Above all that we should not praise or blame Morrison's lyricism without a closer look. In these five examples alone, we get at least three different stylistic moves. The writer borrows a character's perception and mood, her angle of vision, and offers her own language in return — as we saw in our earlier example about the excitement of the neighbors and the reporter. She slips into a character's imagery and lets it speak for itself. And she looks at and names a character's condition, translating not from the character's point of view into the writer's language, but from the writer's point of view into the writer's preferred figure of speech. All three moves are equally valid, of course, although I think the first two work better for Morrison, and certainly, as I now hope to demonstrate, take us deeper into her work.

The instances I have cited are particular and personal, intricately situated and not pretending to objectivity. But none of them is contentious, although a couple of them reflect bitter observations. Even the contentious claims in *Paradise* may seem smoother or more polite than they are, because it is tempting for readers to identify with certain arguments and characters in the novel rather than others, even against others. That is, when a character articulates what we think, or think we think, or would like to think, this version seems to override all others, to belong to a removed realm of truth, and probably to be the author's own view. Now there may be such a realm, but it is not available to any of the characters in *Paradise*, and it is not available to Morrison or to us for much of our lives—not available at all in relation to disputes about race and history and memory. However, it is important to see that the temptation itself is part of Morrison's art. She is not inviting us to an elementary relativism (everything depends upon your point of view); she is asking us to think our principles and prejudices through to the point of whatever resists them.

I find myself wanting to believe, for example, that Patricia the schoolteacher is simply right about the racism of the town where she lives, its scorn for blacks of lighter color than that of its deep-black founding fathers. On their way to establishing their first town in 1890, the fathers were denied entry into a black city in Oklahoma, and this refusal, mimed every year in the town's nativity play, as a whole set of Josephs and Marys is turned away from the inn by people like themselves, is at the heart of the town's ongoing mythology: "Their horror of whites was convulsive but abstract. They saved the clarity of their hatred for the men who had insulted them in ways too confounding for language. . . . Everything anybody wanted to know about the citizens of Haven or Ruby lay in the ramifications of that one rebuff out of many" (189). There is much in the novel to support Patricia's view, and we need to hear what she is saying. But she is wrong in thinking she knows everything we could want to know. Indeed, if we knew only what Patricia knows about Haven or Ruby, we would know almost nothing. We need to remember too that Patricia is not a neutral observer, she is the daughter of a man who married a lighter-skinned woman, and two sentences later, she is looking out of her window at her mother's grave, and seeing the metaphorical sequins we have already encountered. Patricia's view is not invalidated by its context, of course; but it is contextualized.

I am also tempted to believe that Richard Misner, the Baptist minister and a relative newcomer to the town, is simply right about the way the older people in the town are locked into their past: "Over and over and with the least provocation, they pulled from their stock of stories tales about the old folks, their grands and great-grands, their fathers and mothers. . . . Testimonies to endurance, wit, skill and strength. Tales of luck and outrage. But why were there no stories to tell of themselves? About their own lives they shut up. Had nothing to say, pass on" (161). The echo of *Beloved* in the phrase "pass on" alerts us to the importance of the issue, but then again this point of view, couched in something much closer to *style indirect libre*, rich as it is in its partial truth, is distinctly limited and fully situated. Richard is "enraged" by these people (160). He is worried about his own contribution to the town's troubles, because he has been encouraging younger people to speak up. He belongs to a generation marked by the assassinations of Martin Luther King, Jr., and Malcolm X, and he feels the romance of Africa in a way that most of his parishioners do not. "'Africa is our home,'" he says (210), and home is a dream of belonging beyond all conflict and conquest, a version of paradise before the fall: "'I don't mean heaven. I mean a real earthly home. . . . Not some place you went to and invaded and slaughtered people to get. Not some place you claimed, snatched because you got the guns . . . but your own home, where if you go back . . . past the whole of Western history, past the beginnings of organized knowledge, past pyramids and poison bows, on back to when rain was new, before plants forgot they could sing and birds thought they were fish, back when God said Good! Good! — there, right there where you know your own people were born and lived and died'" (213). This is beautiful, but it does not feel like reliable history or politics. Patricia, who is listening to Richard as he gets launched, says, "'You preaching, Reverend.'" He says he is not, he is talking. "'I'm talking to you, Pat'" (213). He is talking and preaching. We do not have to distrust him to know we need to see the world from other angles as well.

A more contorted, more troubling instance: by the end of the novel the upright Steward Morgan has become a cold-blooded killer, and we are right to see him as such. But he is also, at another point, twice said to have "innocent eyes" (156). Who sees his eyes this way? The narrator seems to be re-porting generalized community views at this stage, is not close to any partic-ular character except Steward himself, who is not likely to be thinking of how his eyes look. Is this innocence an illusion, mere appearance? Or is it that a certain kind of stubborn, handsome innocence could drive a man to murder, that Steward is guilty because he is innocent? The tangle of paradox reminds us of other powerful and difficult formulations in Morrison's work: "'If I hadn't killed her, she would have died'" (*Beloved* 200).

These divergent perspectives do not result in the suggestion that all possi-ble interpretations are equal. We need to feel pretty strongly that some of these partial views are sufficient in order to understand why they are not. We are implicated in these affairs, cannot afford to sit back and watch the spectacle as if it was not happening to us. That fiction is something that hap-pens to us, if not (fortunately) as finally as history happens to us, is one of Morrison's most demanding and enabling convictions.

This conviction is everywhere visible in her writing, but it finds especially interesting technical reflections in *Paradise* — in the ease and frequency of flashbacks, for instance, which make old times seem contemporary, and the present seem full of layers: "She crossed Central Avenue toward them. . . . She walked fast. . . . He carried the equipment box through the dining room" (53). These sentences occur in quick succession, but nothing except our own piecing together of the story allows us to identify the first two as part of a memory and the third as current narration. So too in the proffering of the figurative version of an event before the literal one: "Then a mighty hand dug deep into a giant sack and threw fistfuls of petals into the air. Or so it seemed. Butterflies" (90). And in the subtle slippage from waking world to dream and back: "Having misread the warning, she was about to hostess one of the biggest messes Ruby had ever seen. Both of her dead sons were leaning against the Kelvinator, cracking the shells of Spanish peanuts. 'What's that in the sink?' Easter asked her. She looked and saw feathers — brightly col-ored but small like chicken feathers — lying in a heap in her sink. . . . She woke up wondering what kind of bird was colored that way" (154–55). The dead sons are there before there is any indication that this is a dream. The dreamer's first interpretation of the warning is that the feathers refer to the buzzards which have been flying over the town; her second that the strange feathers in the sink indicate that things and people are not in their place. What she cannot possibly know is that her husband's extra-marital affair released in his mistress "the wing of a feathered thing, undead" (226). Even though she has learned of the affair by the time of her dream, she can know only through telepathy, or the echoing magic of fiction, that she and the other women meet up in their imagery.

In all of these cases the freedom of fiction not only permits the imagining of alternatives to the given world, it infiltrates the world itself, reshapes it. It is true the world to be reshaped is fictional, but then the historical world too has often been altered by powerful fictions—of racial superiority among other notable things. The open intervention of fiction within Morrison's fiction is not floating self-reference but a model for the mind's capacity to change what it sees—its real but not limitless capacity.

Does the title of the novel speak of paradise, or of paradises, the plural hidden in the singular, the way multiple perceptions are hidden in the continuity of Morrison's voice? Would there be a way of folding the plural back into the singular? Is paradise, a closed garden in most mythologies, a place of negative purity, as Patricia suspects? A place where bigoted men rule the roost, "good brave men on their way to Paradise," as a voice very close to Patricia's sarcastically thinks (201–02)? Is it a place of peace, as Richard imagines, a cancellation of conquest and empire and violent America? When he thinks of the divided town as a "hard-won heaven" (306), he is remaking it in the image of his own hopes: "How exquisitely human was the wish for permanent happiness, and how thin human imagination became trying to achieve it" (306). Richard thinks he is analyzing the mentality of the town, but he is really converting it into a place he can like better, and can decide to stay in, as he does so decide a sentence or two later. His decision is one of very few weak spots in the novel, and also one of its most beautiful moments—beautiful because of its weakness. Having decided to stay Richard thinks of these people who so recently enraged him—and who even more recently slaughtered a group of harmless women—as "these outrageously beautiful, flawed and proud people" (306). They are beautiful and proud, of course; outrageously beautiful maybe; but to call them, in the light of what they have done, "flawed" is to refuse history for the sake of the future, and Morrison wants us to do better than that, however sympathetic we may be (and perhaps she is) to Richard's view. We have to face the future without refusing history—we have to see what he cannot bear to see.

"I have this creepy sensation . . . of loss," Morrison said in a 1978 interview. "Like something is either lost, never to be retrieved, or something is about to be lost and will never be retrieved" (Mathus 13). The losses in her work have changed over the years, and many of them were not of paradise. But paradise is a wonderful image for what we might call the suspected loss, the fear that loss is what our story will disclose, that loss is what we have. Morrison's suggestion is not quite that the true paradises are lost paradises, as Proust so lucidly suggested (Proust 903); it is that we do not know the name of what we have lost and that paradise is a word which catches our disarray, a word that grieves for us. The murdering Steward Morgan may seem to be the polar opposite of the peace-dreaming Richard Misner, and a long way from paradise, but he too has his vision, none the less compelling for being so stately and hierarchical. Long ago, he and his twin brother Deacon went on a trip with the menfolk of their family. In a prosperous town they saw

nineteen Negro ladies arrange themselves on the steps of the town hall. They wore summer dresses of material the lightness, the delicacy of which neither of them had ever seen. Most of the dresses were white, but two were lemon yellow and one a salmon color. They wore small, pale hats of beige, dusty rose, powdery blue: hats that called attention to the wide, sparkly eyes of the wearers. Their waists were not much bigger than their necks. Laughing and teasing, they preened for a photographer. . . . Deek heard musical voices, low, full of delight and secret information, and in their tow a gust of verbena. . . . Deek's image of the nineteen summertime ladies was unlike the photographer's. His remembrance was pastel colored and eternal. (109–10)

Negro ladies, we note, not black women. Black and white photography, but colored words and memories. It is for such ladies that men of a certain generation might want to build a world. The ladies would be gracious and grateful, would acknowledge the gift and know their place. They would be Eves aloof from temptation—or at least from Eve's temptation to mastery. And it is because they represent a mockery of this memory—for Steward even more than for Deacon—that the murdered women have to die. Paradise can be lethal, an accomplice in crime, particularly for a man with "innocent eyes": "The women . . . were for him a flaunting parody of nineteen Negro ladies of his and his brother's youthful memory and perfect understanding. They were a degradation of that moment they'd shared of sunlit skin and verbena. They, with their mindless giggles, outraged the dulcet tones . . . of the nineteen ladies who, scheduled to live forever in pastel shaded dreams, were now doomed to extinction by this new and obscene breed of female" (279). The language ("mindless"/"dulcet," "pastel"/"obscene," and the brilliantly critical "scheduled") makes clear we are not being asked to endorse this view. But we are being asked to understand it, to see that it contains, in its way, a conflictless dream of grace and honor not unlike Richard's. Morrison's "creepy sensation...of loss" includes the awareness that even the loss of error is still a loss. Or that there are very few enduring errors which are not haunted by truths hard to find elsewhere. So that when the narrator describes the offending women as "bodacious black Eves unredeemed by Mary" (18), she is both miming Steward's view and refuting it. When Connie tells the women that "Eve is Mary's mother" and "Mary is the daughter of Eve" (263), she is denying the difference that means so much to Steward, but remembering that temptation and purity do not ordinarily or easily go together.

I have not yet mentioned the most obvious reference to paradise in the novel, which occurs in its last sentence, and indeed forms its last word. This is a vision not of loss but of homecoming, or of loss redeemed, but then three short words make clear that the difficult historical world has not been abandoned, only momentarily transfigured. An old black woman named Piedade is singing to another, younger black woman who is Connie dead and reborn. They are on a beach, surrounded by gleaming "sea trash." Heaving waves mark the arrival of something, "another ship, perhaps," of which we learn only that it contains "crew and passengers, lost and saved," and that they are "atremble, for they have been disconsolate for some time" (318). "Disconsolate," as Mathus points out, is a lovely pun, since Connie's full name is Consolata, and those who are arriving have lost her and needed her—needed what she is and what she knows (167). The travelers have come, perhaps, from life to the life after death; or have crossed an earthly ocean as slaves or as free people. Either way, they are here, and their subjection is over. But not their labor. And here is "down here," where we are, where we always were. "Now," the book concludes, "they will rest before shouldering the endless work they were created to do down here in Paradise" (318). This is not the paradise of Adam and Eve; it is the paradise they, and we, might have built beyond its gate.

Might have built but did not. "They shoot the white girl first," is how *Paradise* memorably opens. On a July morning of 1976 nine men have arrived at the remote house they call the Convent, determined to eradicate the evil they believe to be represented by the five straying or abandoned women who live there. But it is not until the last but one chapter of the book that the narration of this slaughter is completed, and we learn the names of the men.

In the first chapter they are only shadowy roles and relations haunted by snatches of history, identified only as "the youngest," "the leading man," "his brother," "a father and his son," "the nephew" — as if their names were a secret we have to be ready for, or as if unnamed killers cannot kill. Finally we see them shoot two women indoors, and we hear one of the men say they have shot the other three as they ran across a clover field. But mysteriously, at the end of the chapter, there are no bodies inside or outside, and even the women's car, an ancient Cadillac, is gone.

What has happened? The novel itself is rife with speculation. There are "two editions of the official story": the men went out to the Convent, there was a fight, "the women took other shapes and disappeared into thin air"; the men went out to the Convent, there was a fight, and one woman, the oldest, was killed by "some" of the men (296–97). Patricia, who is passing on these versions to Richard Misner, has her own firm theory: nine coal-black men murdered five harmless women because the women were either not black or not black enough, because the women were "unholy," and "because they could" — because they felt they belonged to a black world above the law (297). But then what happened to the bodies? The town midwife, also a psychic, who knew what was going to happen and arrived at the Convent in time to witness the tail end of it, including two bodies, is distressed by the way everyone tells a different version of the story, but settles for an acceptance of God's will: "God had given Ruby a second chance. Had made Himself so visible and unarguable a presence that even the outrageously prideful... and the uncorrectably stupid... ought to be able to see it. He had actually swept up and received His servants in broad daylight..." (297–98). One of the young women in the town has a more down-to-earth story: " 'One of them or maybe more wasn't dead. Nobody actually looked — they just assumed. Then... they got the hell out of there. Taking the killed ones with them. Simple, right?' " (303–04) But then this same young woman, out at the Convent, suddenly sees what she calls a door into what may be another world: "What would be on the other side? What on earth would it be? What on earth?" (305) We know that the women at the Convent have practiced magic, black or white according to your point of judgment, and that one of them has the power to raise the dead.

If the novel ended here, we could perhaps settle for the way these versions correct and refute and corroborate each other — although even then we would need to emphasize the unmistakable dead bodies and their equally unmistakable vanishing. But the novel has a short epilogue following on from these events and interpretations, in which each of the women is seen revisiting her life, in all cases but one reconciled to a loved one before she returns to wherever she is going. Are these figures ghosts, dreams? This is precisely the question we do not have to answer in fiction, where ghosts and dreams are the original inhabitants. Are the women dead? Probably, or as dead as fictional characters can get. Are they alive after death? Of course, they are there in front of us on the page, talking, swimming, looking for a favorite pair of shoes, eating grits and eggs, falling on glass. What more could a live body do?

There are all kinds of ways of thinking about this situation. Much depends on our own actual beliefs about death and what follows death. At the very least we are being asked, not to solve a difficult puzzle, but to reflect on the way fiction and memory resemble and reinforce each other, and the way both of them, inestimable consolations that they are, will also betray us if we let them. To say, for example, that fiction is fantasy or magic and nothing more, that the dead are alive if we think they are, or that active remembering abolishes death, is to reach for a comfort that will quickly fade, and that actually diminishes the horror and dignity of death, to say nothing of the crime of murder. But to say that the dead are just dead, that all possibilities end with the end of bodily life, is to miss the ongoing power of memory, and the ability of fiction to engage with the very loss it cannot deny. "They will live/and they will not die again," is what is promised to believers in the Gnostic Gospels, and cited by Morrison in the novel's epigraph. Memory promises the same: an acceptance of the first death is the condition for the avoidance of the second. But fiction's promise is slightly different. Its characters are promised that they will live, and they will die. And they will live again, and die again, and again and again, as long as there are readers who believe in them. Their voices will speak and clash, their moral persuasions will make their claims on us, and the assembly of their styles will form, as Bakhtin says, the language of the novel.

The dead and alive women of the epilogue to *Paradise*, like a number of other figures in Morrison's fiction, are pictures of possibility, of second chances. And they are reminders that possibilities themselves, outside of fiction, are often canceled by the intractable real, that for many people the first chance is also the last. The dialogue between this acknowledgment and the imagined alternative is what matters. Fiction cannot restore our losses but it can get us beyond their helpless reenactment.

MEDITATIONS ON
A BIRD IN THE HAND
Ethics and Aesthetics
in a Parable by Toni Morrison

Cheryl Lester

My reflections on aesthetic ideology in Toni Morrison's Nobel Prize Lecture appear in what follows as a form of call-and-response, staying very much
in the neighborhood and spirit and order of the Lecture. They engage and
resonate with the aesthetic principles foregrounded in the Lecture rather than
being organized around them. Therefore, it may help to offer an overview of
these principles before turning to my reflections on the Lecture itself. First
and foremost is Morrison's insistence that language and its productions are
acts rather than products or artifacts. Using language is thus equivalent to
performing particular, situated actions, aimed at particular audiences, for
specific purposes, with specific effects. Now, language use can be ethical or
unethical. Language used ethically may have any or all of the following aims:
it may be used to grapple with meaning, express love, or provide guidance.

For the purpose of ethical action, Morrison believes that language users
should aim to express the historical specificity of their knowledge and experience, should place truth before beauty, and should recognize their expressive activity as a moral imperative. The longstanding dominance of market
values notwithstanding, Morrison's aesthetic principles suggest that language
offers an economy and a site where non-market values such as love, wisdom,
and guidance can be sustained and transmitted. Storytelling serves as an apt

figure for Morrison's belief that language use can animate or stifle meaningful relationships with others, ourselves, and our past.

As I drove around New Orleans in my friend Carrie's car listening to Toni Morrison delivering her Nobel Prize Lecture (not the same thing, I see from my xeroxed pages of the slim and too expensive Knopf edition, as her Acceptance Speech), I started to cry.

Narrative has never been merely entertainment for me. It is, I believe, one of the principal ways in which we absorb knowledge.

I was finally in New Orleans. Carrie had just moved there, from Kansas, and I was there to gather at a conference with the three other women who had organized the Quindaro Oral History Project in Kansas City, Kansas, in summer 1996. One of these women had taken my picture the day after my father died and sent it to me with the title "Woman in Grief," but I suspected she meant "Co-Director of NEH Summer Seminar in Grief When She Was Supposed To Be Working." Throughout that summer, my attention was divided, between my father's battle to recover from triple bypass surgery just enough to undergo an operation on stomach cancer and . . .

I hope you will understand, then, why I begin these remarks with the opening phrase of what must be the oldest sentence in the world, and the earliest one we remember from childhood: "Once upon a time . . ."

My father saw Kansas for the first time in April, riding in a wheelchair-accessible van from the airport to Lawrence. He had been in Harper Hospital in Detroit since the first week of January, mostly in the Intensive Care Unit, where we celebrated his eightieth birthday. He'd had a dual-lead pacemaker installed in December; there'd been problems with the installation — loss of blood, a lead left unconnected — and thus began the first of a hundred Doctor talks. "If it were *my* father," they often said, hurriedly glancing at the chart, with little or no idea what the last specialist had thought, or done, or forgotten to do, or whose problem my father would be tomorrow. Viewing the Kansas fields and livestock and sunshine, my father beamed, muttering blessings over those who had helped him survive the past hundred days and nights and curses at those who had failed to visit, call, or even send a card. He was not happy to be heading for a nursing home. "Why can't I stay by you?" he pleaded. For the tenth time, I reminded him that he couldn't walk, go up or down stairs, be alone all day in my house. As soon as he could walk up and down stairs, he would come "by us."

"Once upon a time there was an old woman. Blind but wise." Or was it an old man? A guru perhaps. Or a griot soothing restless children. I have heard this story, or one exactly like it, in the lore of several cultures.

I know this is not the place to talk about my father's death. Yet somehow, trying to understand why I started to cry as I listened to Toni Morrison's Nobel Prize Lecture, the contradictions of that summer assert themselves. The NEH Summer Seminar on African-American Migration and American Culture. The Quindaro Oral History Project. My father.... And I want to let them stand, since they insist, as an entryway to my thoughts about Morrison's lecture, on the occasion of her acceptance of the Nobel Prize.

Once upon a time there was an old woman. Blind. Wise.

At this point in the lecture, I'm sure I wasn't crying yet. I was intrigued that Morrison had decided to respond to this occasion by telling a story, begging the understanding of her audience — "Members of the Swedish Academy, Ladies and Gentlemen" — as she gently shifted them from one set of expectations to another.

I hope you will understand, then, why I begin these remarks with the opening phrase of what must be the oldest sentence in the world, and the earliest one we remember from childhood: "Once upon a time . . ."

Morrison reminds her audience that storytelling is as old as the sun, crucial to the formation of societies as well as subjects, worthy of our respect and emulation. Storytelling may well be, she argues, among our most enduring recollections and primal scenes of learning. Interweaving the conventions of storytelling with the conventions of lecturing, Morrison continues the didactic thrust of her opening assertion. *"Narrative,"* she stated at the outset, *"has never been merely entertainment for me. It is, I believe, one of the principal ways in which we absorb knowledge."* On this occasion, then, her turn to storytelling promises to convey some particular knowledge to her audience but also to reflect upon and measure the modes in which we convey and absorb knowledge today.

Taking as her point of departure a story whose superior wisdom is indicated by the fact that it is common to the lore of several cultures, Morrison indicates her belief in the primacy of storytelling as a way of conveying and absorbing knowledge. Toward the conclusion of her lecture, she enlarges upon the particulars of her version of the story, but for now, she focuses on the story as a scenic representation of the context in which wisdom is conveyed and learning takes place.

In the version I know the woman is the daughter of slaves, black, American, and lives alone in a small house outside of town. Her reputation for wisdom is without peer and without question. Among her people she is both the law and its transgression. The honor she is paid and the awe in which she is held reach beyond her neighborhood to places far away; to the city where the intelligence of rural prophets is the source of much amusement.

One day the woman is visited by some young people who seem to be bent on disproving her clairvoyance and showing her up for the fraud they believe she is. Their plan is simple: they enter her house and ask the one question the answer to which rides solely on her difference from them, a difference they regard as a profound disability: her blindness. They stand before her, and one of them says,

"Old woman, I hold in my hand a bird. Tell me whether it is living or dead." She does not answer, and the question is repeated. "Is the bird I am holding living or dead?"

Still she does not answer. She is blind and cannot see her visitors, let alone what is in their hands. She does not know their color, gender or homeland. She only knows their motive.

The old woman's silence is so long, the young people have trouble holding their laughter.

Finally she speaks, and her voice is soft but stern. "I don't know," she says. "I don't know whether the bird you are holding is dead or alive, but what I do know is that it is in your hands. It is in your hands."

By telling this story, Morrison assumes the position of the wise old storyteller, and she places her distinguished audience in the place of the inquiring children who have come to visit her. Perhaps her audience, like those children, want proof of Morrison's wisdom, answers to their questions. In response to this demand, real or imaginary, Morrison turns her lecture into a reflecting pool, inviting us to consider and reconsider both her position and our own. Does she really resemble the old blind woman? Do we resemble the children? Dizzy already, I wonder why Morrison settled on this particular analogy, with its emphasis on the face-to-face encounter, particularly on the mythic encounter of the young and old. I have been persuaded by the arguments about modernity and postmodernity as conditions marked by the proliferation and sanctification of information and the disappearance of those human relationships that nourish and transmit wisdom. Does Morrison's opening gambit betray ineffectual nostalgia for a kind of knowledge and mode of transmission that are obsolete, beyond hope of resurrection?

To answer this question, we have to examine the *explication de texte* that composes the bulk of Morrison's lecture. She begins her lengthy commentary by specifying that she reads the bird in the hand as language and the old woman as a practiced writer. Speaking from the perspective of the old woman, she draws an elaborate distinction between living and dead language. Speaking next from the perspective of the children, she articulates the demands, desires, and needs that dictate the old woman's responsibilities as a writer.

It might have been when Morrison said that that bird stood for language that I started to cry. Suddenly feeling as if she were talking specifically to me. With those children standing there with "language" in their hands, waiting to hear whether it was dead or alive, I already began to think that it was me — teacher, wordworker, counselor — whose responsibilities were in question. Having created a scenario in which what seemed to be in question were Morrison's qualifications for the honor and distinction she was about to receive, it was now her listeners — brokers big or small of authority, power, knowledge, and language — who had to measure themselves as well. We, Morrison's audience, were no longer positioned in the inquiring place of the young people. Now we stood with Morrison in the weighty place of the old blind woman.

Signifying on the story she recited as well as on the maxim she did not — "a bird in the hand is worth two in the bush" — Morrison sermonizes, reminding those who hold language in their hands that power, agency, and responsibility are not elsewhere; they are in our hands. Listening to Morrison's vivid excoriation of lethal language, I was forced inward to reflect on my own language usage. Like the young Stephen Daedalus at a Catholic school retreat, I heard accusations in every assertion, especially as Morrison, speaking in the voice of the old woman, elaborated on the ways in which users can kill language and at the same time render it deadly to others.

Being a writer, she thinks of language partly as a system, partly as a living thing over which one has control, but mostly as agency — as an act with consequences. So the question the children put to her, "Is it living or dead?," is not unreal, because she thinks of language as susceptible to death, erasure; certainly imperiled and salvageable only by an effort of the will.

Morrison's claim that language is imperiled, susceptible to death and erasure, is not primarily addressed to the destiny of languages like Aramaic, Latin, or

Ancient Greek, which are no longer the spoken or written expression of a living people. Rather her claim is addressed to *unyielding language*, language — and here begins her unremitting deployment of hail and brimstone — *language content to admire its own paralysis*. Medusa-like, unyielding language is like official language, the restrictive and restricting language of the state, but it is more broadly *censored and censoring*, rendered mute and rendering mute what Morrison has elsewhere called the unspeakable unspoken. As Morrison went on, I came increasingly to see the implication of my acts, or failures to act, in connection with the death and erasure of language.

Ruthless in its policing duties, it has no desire or purpose other than to maintain the free range of its own narcotic narcissism, its own exclusivity and dominance. However moribund, it is not without effect, for it actively thwarts the intellect, stalls conscience, suppresses human potential. Unreceptive to interrogation, it cannot form or tolerate new ideas, shape other thoughts, tell another story, fill baffling silences.

Listening to the recording of this lecture, I felt myself a target of Morrison's anger, guilty of wrongs I habitually attributed to others. I thought uncomfortably of my role in the classroom and at home as a foot soldier in the army of ideological state apparachniks, however assiduously I strive to subvert the forward march of self-satisfied personal and social narratives. I recalled times when my language had stifled interrogation, or been useless to others with another story to tell, another baffled silence to fill with sound and meaning.

She is convinced that when language dies, out of carelessness, disuse, indifference, and absence of esteem, or killed by fiat, not only she herself but all users and makers are accountable for its demise.

There are countless ways to kill language, and Morrison includes ordinary attitudes such as *carelessness, disuse, indifference, and absence of esteem*. I was stunned at her suggestion that you also kill language by failing to esteem yourself. Perhaps it prevents you from acting according to your ability. When it is necessary to act, modesty and humility can be set aside but perhaps absence of esteem is not so easily overcome. Morrison's awareness of such inadvertent contributions to the evacuation of language explains her belief that, when language is evacuated, *all users and makers are accountable*. No one, no adult, is innocent unless she or he is breathing life into language by vigilantly *grappling with meaning, providing guidance, or expressing love*.

Academics often oppose themselves to the oppressive language of the state, yet Morrison accuses academic language (*proud but calcified*) of being lethally oppressive, of failing to enliven language by using it to grapple with meaning, provide guidance, or express love. The *intellectual mercenary* is no better than the *insatiable dictator*, the *paid-for politician or demagogue*, or the *counterfeit journalist, and the old woman is keenly aware* that she is unlikely to persuade any of these wordworkers to interrogate or reform their practice. Perhaps Morrison's desire to try to persuade them nevertheless explains why she redoubles her efforts at precisely this point by amplifying upon the lethal violence of their language acts and by highlighting the guilt of scholarly language.

There is and will be rousing language to keep citizens armed and arming; slaughtered and slaughtering in the malls, courthouses, post offices, playgrounds, bedrooms and boulevards; stirring, memorializing language to mask the pity and waste of needless death. There will be more diplomatic language to countenance rape, torture, assassination. There is and will be more seductive, mutant language designed to throttle women, to pack their throats like pate-producing geese with their own unsayable, transgressive words; there will be more of the language of surveillance disguised as research; of politics and history calculated to render the suffering of millions mute; language glamorized to thrill the dissatisfied and bereft into assaulting their neighbors; arrogant pseudo-empirical language crafted to lock creative people into cages of inferiority and hopelessness.

Underneath the eloquence, the glamour, the scholarly associations, however stirring or seductive, the heart of such language is languishing, or perhaps not beating at all—if the bird is already dead.

She has thought about what could have been the intellectual history of any discipline if it had not insisted upon, or been forced into, the waste of time and life that rationalizations for and representations of dominance required—lethal discourses of exclusion blocking access to cognition for both the excluder and the excluded.

Here, feeling both perpetrator and victim, I choke at the cost (*the waste of time and life that rationalizations for and representations of dominance required*) of what I have endeavored to say (throat packed *like a pate-producing goose with unsayable, transgressive words*) and of what I have not mustered the tongue or heart to utter. Whose insistence supports our enthrallment to this mutant language? How is it en-forced? How can we extract ourselves from the suffocating hold of lethal language? What is the harm of speaking Other-Wise? Morrison encourages us to use our idiosyncratic tongues, to embrace rather than abhor a multiplicity of languages. The old woman challenges conventional wisdom with an alternative reading of the Tower of Babel, arguing that we should rejoice in its collapse.

Perhaps the achievement of Paradise was premature, a little hasty if no one could take the time to understand other languages, other views, other narratives. Had they, the heaven they imagined might have been found at their feet.

Vital language, the old woman wants her young audience to know, does not fix meaning; it does not even point toward meaning; rather, she believes, it *arcs toward the places where meaning may lie.* She believes that the vitality of language lies in its reach toward human lives, in its ability to stretch, not with pride but deference, toward *the actual, imagined and possible lives of its speakers, readers, writers.* She cites the Gettysburg Address to demonstrate how language can be used to sustain rather than molest life with arrogance and pride.

When a President of the United States thought about the graveyard his country had become, and said, "The world will little note nor long remember what we say here. But it will never forget what they did here," his simple words were exhilarating in their life-sustaining properties because they refused to encapsulate the reality of 600,000 dead men in a cataclysmic race war. Refusing to monumentalize, disdaining the "final word," the precise "summing up," acknowledging their "poor power to add or detract," his words signal deference to the uncapturability of the life it mourns.

Morrison's example is far from accidental, for it returns us to the particular history and life of the old woman, blind, wise, black, American, and the daughter of slaves. She, Morrison imagines, is moved by President Lincoln's famous address, moved above all by the deference to life he showed in his refusal to use language to *"pin down"* slavery, genocide, war. Stating that unmolested language *surges toward knowledge, not its destruction,* Morrison's old woman condemns the proud declarations and laborious proofs of scholarly argumentation in favor of the interrogative, critical, and alternative thrusts of living language.

Word-work is sublime, she thinks, because it is generative; it makes meaning that secures our difference, our human difference — the way in which we are like no other life.
We die. That may be the meaning of life. But we do language. That may be the measure of our lives.

Funny, for all the rousing exhortations spoken through her mouth, the old woman is not left intact as the perfect embodiment of living language. As

Morrison turns to the old woman's young visitors, we discover what the old woman's solitary existence may have allowed her to forget, namely, that language languishes in isolation. For language to live and flourish, Morrison counsels us, it must enter into human relationships. Returning to the scene of her parable, Morrison reexamines the young people's demand and the old woman's response. She hypothesizes that the young visitors had no bird in their hands and came instead for the *chance to interrupt, to violate the adult world, its miasma of discourse about them.* Having come to establish a relationship with the adult world, which has failed to take them seriously, the children are angry at the old woman, who ignored or overlooked their wish to connect with her as their elder.

She keeps her secret, her good opinion of herself; her gnomic pronouncements, her art without commitment. She keeps her distance, enforces it and retreats into the singularity of isolation, in sophisticated, privileged space.

The young visitors' criticism seems apt, yet her silence has a notably generative effect, for they begin to *fill it with language invented on the spot.* They accuse her of withholding her wisdom from them out of indifference, pride, selfishness, or forgetfulness, and they exhort her to take responsibility for them, for their future.

> *Do we have to begin consciousness with a battle heroes and heroines like you have already fought and lost, leaving us with nothing in our hands except what you have imagined is there?*
> *. . . Is there no context for our lives? No song, no literature, no poem full of vitamins, no history connected to experience that you can pass along to help us start strong? You are an adult. The old one, the wise one. Stop thinking about saving your face. Think of our lives and tell us your particularized world. Make up a story. Narrative is radical, creating us at the very moment it is being created. We will not blame you if your reach exceeds your grasp; if love so ignites your words that they go down in flames and nothing is left but their scald. . . . For our sake and yours forget your name in the street, tell us what the world has been to you in the dark places and in the light. Don't tell us what to believe, what to fear. Show us belief's wide skirt and the stitch that unravels fear's caul.*

What the visitors demand with so much passion seems simple: *tell us what the world has been to you.* Yet their passion for knowing belies the fact that they have been told so little. Believing that it is pride that keeps the old woman from telling them the truth of her particularized world, they beg her to stop thinking about *saving face,* to forget her *name in the street.* If the price of recognition is *tongue-suicide*, Morrison's youngsters assert, then it is worth losing face, worth risking your name on the street. They will praise her for finding her tongue, for speaking frankly and truly of fear and belief, life and death, what the world has been to her.

"Tell us what it is to be a woman so that we may know what it is to be a man. What moves at the margin. What it is to have no home in this place. To be set adrift from the one you knew. What it is to live at the edge of towns that cannot bear your company."

Almost imperceptibly, the visitor's importations arc toward a story of their own, the story they imagine she could tell them, if she would. The story is about a wagonload of slaves, headed toward enslavement. The children focus on details of the journey, especially on the thirst of the slaves and the water they receive at a stop along the way, perhaps the last they will know of human kindness. When the children finish, the old woman breaks the silence, and her final words to them are also the final words of Morrison's lecture.

"Finally," she says. "I trust you now. I trust you with the bird that is not in your hands because you have truly caught it. Look. How lovely it is, this thing we have done—together."

In the end, wise as she is, the old woman transforms the children's criticism into proof of her wisdom, for her silence encouraged them to use their tongues, to speak their yearning. What Morrison asks of wordworkers is, first, to trust enough to tell their audience what the world has been to them and, second, to create an opening, a space, a hearing for other tongues untied.

Papa Neely and my father both died that summer. Papa Neely, at home in Quindaro; my father, back at the nursing home. Papa Neely was around a hundred years old, though no one knew his exact age, and many people in Quindaro hoped he would consent to be interviewed for the Oral History Project. Perhaps they knew his stories, or perhaps they only wished he would tell them. By chance, I met his daughter, and she invited me to the house. Within minutes, however, and in spite of his daughter's prodding, Papa Neely made it plain that he had nothing to say to me. He pretended he didn't understand my questions or couldn't remember the answers. Standing at his bedside, I was certain that he was shining me on. Whatever interest I might have in listening to his story, there was nothing he wished to communicate to me, and no reason why he should make any effort on my behalf. I was a stranger and, what's more, I was white. He made me feel ineradicably white.

My father lived nearly four months in Kansas, at the nursing home, at my house, and in the hospital. Bitter and helpless, he spent most of his final months of life complaining about food. Whoever prepared it, them or me, it was not to his liking. Too hot or too cold, too tough or too lean, his food lacked flavor, heartiness, sweetness. Undercooked or overcooked, underripe or overripe, nothing seemed edible. He was ordered to watch his diet, until they found cancer in his prostrate. The surgeon was willing to perform the operation if my father could put on some weight and strengthen his muscles. By this time, however, my father no longer had an appetite. All that focus on food—on shopping, preparing, and storing—all the orders and complaints were smokescreens, designed to hide the fact that his cancer had gotten the upper hand.

By mid-May, after he'd grown strong enough to come "by us," he had come to believe he just might hang on for a few more years. It may have been the discovery of his prostate cancer that took away his will to live, or it may have been that he didn't feel sufficiently needed or loved. With the Seminar and the Oral History Project, I was too busy to stay with him often enough or long enough. Perhaps that was why he spent our time sending me away to shop and cook food he could no longer eat. Perhaps he trusted me with his stories no more than Papa Neely did. Yet if so, it was not because I was a stranger or because I was white. Perhaps it was my womanhood that prevented him from speaking to me truly. Perhaps it was too difficult to break a lifetime's habit of keeping the truth to himself.

Still recovering from "post-pump psychosis" after the bypass surgery, my father wanted to tell me the circumstances of his divorce from my mother thirty-six years earlier. He believed that I blamed and resented him for their separation and that this had been the cause of the tension and strain in our relationship. At the conclusion of his story, he told me that my mother had never really loved him and that they had been a mismatch. "What is love, really?" I asked him, disappointed and upset, still waiting for my father to tell me the truth, still blinded to the fact that this was his truth.

It was May or June already when I drove my father to Kansas City to observe Shabbat at Chabad House. On the way there, my father predicted he would be called to the Torah. Before he mentioned it, I hadn't given it any thought, and I was surprised to learn that it was on his mind, a source of pride as well as anxiety. Although we sat on separate sides of the synagogue, I could easily hear my father crying during his Aliyah, struggling through the prayers. After the hard morning, after lunch with Rabbi Mendy, after his nap and before sundown, we headed back to Lawrence, and my father told me why, shortly after his bar mitzvah, he had stopped going to shul with his father. One Shabbat he stepped outside during services. As he stood on the porch of the synagogue, some neighborhood boys on bicycles began to carry on loudly. Whoever came out to see about the noise assumed my father was guilty as well, and he said as much to the Rabbi, who passed this shameful news on to my grandfather. An impulsive and tyrannical man, my grandfather boxed the ears of his eldest son immediately and in front of everyone, never giving my father a chance to tell his side of the story. I was as shocked to hear this story for the first time as I was to learn what my father had sacrificed to his pride. Was it pride as well that had kept him from sharing the truth of his world with any of his five children? That had made him talk to us — loudly and at length — of anything and everything but?

Today I realize that it was my pride and not his that nourished our silences. Reflecting back on the stories my father did manage to tell, without failing to remind me that he might have told me more had I given more of myself to him, I recognize that it was I who needed to loosen my tongue. I might have upbraided him, as the youngsters upbraided the old woman in Morrison's parable. Like them, I might have implored him to speak, enabling him to see how much I expected from him, and how much more I needed to know. I might have tried to explain that the stories he had passed on to me — painful recollections of injustice, error, and loss — would be blessings to me. That what he had told me about his father's work — overseeing fruit orchards in Poland and carrying full carcasses of beef from slaughterhouse to butcher shops in upstate New York — helped me to understand his own lifelong obsession with meat, animal parts, and butcher's cuts, just as they beautified his love and knowledge of the various seasons and breeds and qualities of fruit. I might have seen my way to sharing his disdain for the psychologist who drove from Topeka to Lawrence to meet with the elderly residents of the nursing home. "The man isn't interested in me," my father said, after their second session. "He's just collecting stories for a book!"

Had I really understood the urgency, I might have stopped driving to Quindaro, stopped driving up the hill to the Hall Center for the Humanities to meet with the NEH Seminar on African-American Migration and American Culture. Now my father's orders, complaints, and indirections appear to me as clumsy overtures foreclosed by my own stiff tongue. Like the red roses he asked a nurse to buy on her brief lunchbreak, so that he could give them to me for my forty-fourth birthday, his demanding postures were all he could muster. Had I spoken to and beyond these postures, I might have quickened the bird I held so briefly in my hands.

Morrison's Nobel Prize lecture exhorts us to think more about wisdom than knowledge. It reminds us — despite the conditions of postmodernism, and despite the increasing dominance of information and instrumental knowledge as market commodities — of the enduring non-market value of wisdom, relating it to the prevailing worth of guidance and love. Morrison embeds these values in human relationships, especially those between young and old, and especially those close kinship and ethnic relationships that link one generation to the next with the complex bond called love. Without trying to speak here to the complexity of love, I invoke it because of its significance to the erotic ethics figured as the lesson of Morrison's parable, which addresses its audience as bearers not of one but two positions of responsibility.

Neither aged nor underage, Morrison's audience is sandwiched between youth and old age; in relationships that cast them as both young and old, we can and should learn two lessons from the parable. As elders, we must learn to avoid fear and denial that lead us to bore the young with platitudes, finding it within our power to reach out, touch, and linger with the young. By giving them our attention, we might learn what they know and want to know, who they are and wish to be, and how they imagine us and our significance to them. Listening to loved ones is often as hard as speaking to them — this is one of love's disturbing complexities, but only by fighting our resistances and theirs, only by learning to listen to our young can we place something in their hands besides what we have imagined is there. At the same time, still having elders ourselves, we must share our attention not only with the young but also with the old. As their youngsters, we must act more courageously to speak, to win a proper hearing, and to listen in turn. In between the commands and complaints and denials, we must insist on telling our elders who we are and what they have been to us. Rare as such open speaking and hearing may be, it is surely how wisdom is produced: when young and old come together, hear one another speak, and recognize that each is speaking his or her own truth. This relationship between young and old is the source of magic, and like all things magic, not easily won. Although our loved ones, young and old, may push us away, and although the pretentious importance of our lives is distracting, we should drop everything to tend to the bird we have in hand.

WORKS CITED

Abrams, M. H. *Doing Things with Texts: Essays in Criticism and Critical Theory*. Ed. Michael Fischer, New York: W. W. Norton and Company, 135–58.

Arensberg, Mary. "Introduction." *The American Sublime*. Ed. Mary Arensberg. Albany: State University of New York Press, 1986. 1–20.

Aristotle. *Nicomachean Ethics*. Trans. H. Rackham. Cambridge: Harvard University Press, 1994.

———. *On the Soul, Parva Naturalia, On Breath*. Trans. W. S. Hett. Cambridge: Harvard University Press, 1975.

Ashe, Bertram D. "'Why Don't He Like My Hair?' Constructing African-American Standards of Beauty in Toni Morrison's *Song of Solomon* and Zora Neale Hurston's *Their Eyes Were Watching God*." *African American Review* 29:4 (1995): 579–92.

Baker, Houston A., Jr. *Afro-American Poetics: Revisions of Harlem and the Black Aesthetic*. Madison: University of Wisconsin Press, 1988.

———. *Blues, Ideology, and Afro-American Literature: A Vernacular Theory*. Chicago: University of Chicago Press, 1984.

———. "Generational Shifts and the Recent Criticism of Afro-American Literature." *Within the Circle: An Anthology of African American Literary Criticism from the Harlem Renaissance to the Present*. Ed. Angelyn Mitchell. Durham: Duke University Press, 1994. 282–328.

———. *The Journey Back: Issues in Black Literature and Criticism*. Chicago: University of Chicago Press, 1980.

———. "When Lindbergh Sleeps with Bessie Smith: The Writing of Place in Toni Morrison's *Sula*." *The Difference Within: Feminism and Critical Theory*. Eds. Elizabeth Meese and Alice Parker. Amsterdam: John Benjamins, 1989. 85–113.

Baker, Houston A., Jr., and Patricia Redmond. "Introduction." *Afro-American Literary Study in the* 1990's. Eds. Houston A. Baker, Jr., and Patricia Redmond. Chicago: University of Chicago Press, 1989. 1–11.

Bakerman, Jane. "The Seams Can't Show: An Interview with Toni Morrison." Taylor-Guthrie 30–42.

Bakhtin, Mikhail. *Rabelais and His World.* Trans. Helene Iswolsky. Bloomington: Indiana University Press, 1984.

Barasch, Frances K. *The Grotesque: A Study in Meanings.* The Hague: Mouton, 1971.

Benjamin, Walter. "The Storyteller." *Illuminations.* Ed. Hannah Arendt. New York: Schocken Books, 1977. 83–109.

Bjork, Patrick-Bryce. *The Novels of Toni Morrison: The Search for Self and Place Within the Community.* New York: Peter Lang, 1994.

Bloom, Harold. *Agon: Towards a Theory of Revisionism.* Oxford: Oxford University Press, 1982.

———. "Emerson and Whitman: The American Sublime." *Poetry and Repression: Revisionism from Blake to Stevens.* New Haven: Yale University Press, 1976. 235–66.

———. "Introduction." *Poets of Sensibility and the Sublime.* Ed. Bloom. New York: Chelsea House, 1986. 1–9.

———. "Introduction." *Toni Morrison.* Ed. Bloom. New York: Chelsea House, 1990. 1–5.

Borghini, Vincenzio. "Selva di notizie." *Scritti d'arte del cinquecento.* Ed. Paoloa Barocchi. Vol. 3: Pittura e Scultura. Turin: Giulio Einaudi Editore, 1978. 637.

Bowers, Susan. "*Beloved* and the New Apocalypse." *The Journal of Ethnic Studies* (1990): 59–77.

Bundles, A'lelia Perry. *Madam C. J. Walker.* Philadelphia: Chelsea House, 1991.

Burke, Edmund. *A Philosophical Enquiry into the Origin of Our Ideas of the Sublime and Beautiful.* Ed. James T. Boulton. London, 1958.

Busby, Mark. *Ralph Ellison.* Boston: Twayne, 1991.

Byerman, Keith E. "Intense Behaviors: The Use of the Grotesque in *The Bluest Eye* and *Eva's Man.*" *CLA Journal* 25 (1982): 447–57.

Callahan, John F. *In the African-American Grain.* Urbana: University of Illinois Press, 1988.

Christian, Barbara. "Community and Nature: The Novels of Toni Morrison." *The Journal of Ethnic Studies* 7:4 (1980): 65–78.

Cixous, Hélène. "Castration or Decapitation?" Trans. Annette Kuhn. *Signs* 7:11 (1981): 52.

Clark, Norris. "Flying Black: Toni Morrison's *The Bluest Eye, Sula,* and *Song of Solomon.*" *Minority Voices* 4.2 (1980): 51–63.

Cleage, Pearl. "Hairpeace." *African American Review* 27:1 (1993): 37–41.

Cliff, Michelle. "I Found God in Myself, and I Loved Her/I Loved Her Fiercely: More Thoughts on the Work of Black Women Artists." *Journal of Feminist Studies in Religion* 2:1 (1986): 7–39.

Cohn, Jan, and Thomas H. Miles. "The Sublime: In Alchemy, Aesthetics and Psychoanalysis." *Modern Philology* 74 (1977): 289–304.

Coleman, James. "Beyond the Reach of Love and Caring: Black Life in Toni Morrison's *Song of Solomon*. *Obsidian II* 1 (1986): 151–61.

Coleman, Willi M. "Among the Things that Use to Be." *Home Girls: A Black Feminist Anthology*. Ed. Barbara Smith. New York: Kitchen Table/Women of Color Press, 1983. 21–22.

Conner, Marc C. "Postmodern Exhaustion: Thomas Pynchon's *Vineland* and the Aesthetic of the Beautiful." *Studies in American Fiction* 24:1 (1996): 65–85.

———. "Wild Women and Graceful Girls: Toni Morrison's Winter's Tale." *Nature, Woman, and the Art of Politics*. Ed. Eduardo Velasquez. Landam, MD: Rowman and Littlefield, 1999. 335–63.

"Conversation with Alice Childress and Toni Morrison." Taylor-Guthrie 3–9.

Cowart, David. "Faulkner and Joyce in Morrison's *Song of Solomon*." *American Literature* 62 (1990): 87–100.

Darling, Marsha. "In the Realm of Responsibility: A Conversation with Toni Morrison." Taylor-Guthrie 246–54.

Davis, Charles T. "The Mixed Heritage of the Modern Black Novel." *Modern Critical Views: Ralph Ellison*. Ed. Harold Bloom. New York: Chelsea, 1986. 101–11.

Davis, Christina. "An Interview with Toni Morrison." Taylor-Guthrie 223–33.

Davis, Cynthia. "Self, Society, and Myth in Toni Morrison's Fiction." *Contemporary Literature* 23:3 (1982): 323–42.

Davis, Marianna. *Contributions of Black Women to America*. Vol. 1. Columbia, South Carolina: Kenday Press, 1982.

Davis, Ossie. "The Language Is My Enemy." *Revelations*. Ed. Tersa M. Redd. Massachusetts: Ginn, 1991. 3.

De Man, Paul. "Phenomenality and Materiality in Kant." *The Textual Sublime: Deconstruction and Its Differences*. Eds. Hugh Silverman and Gary Aylesworth. Albany: State University of New York Press, 1990. 87–108.

Denard, Carolyn. "The Convergence of Feminism and Ethnicity in the Fiction of Toni Morrison." McKay, *Critical Essays*. 171–79.

De Weever, Jacqueline. *Mythmaking and Metaphor in Black Women's Fiction*. New York: St. Martin's Press, 1991.

Diderot, Denis. *Lettre sur les sourds et muets*. Ed. Paul Hugo Meyer. Geneva: Librairie Droz, 1965.

Dillard, J. L. *Black English*. New York: Vantage, 1972.

Doty, Robert M. *Human Concern/Personal Torment: The Grotesque in American Art*. New York: Praeger, 1969.

———. *"human concern/personal torment: the Grotesque in American Art" Revisited*. New York: n.p., 1989.

Du Bois, W. E. B. "Criteria of Negro Art." *W. E. B. Du Bois: Writings*. Ed. Nathan Irvin Huggins. New York: Library of America, 1986. 993–1002.

Duvall, John. "Toni Morrison and the Anxiety of Faulknerian Influence." Kolmerton, *Unflinching Gaze* 3–16.

Eagleton, Terry. *The Ideology of the Aesthetic*. Oxford: Basil Blackwell, 1990.

Ellison, Ralph. "The World and the Jug." *Shadow and Act*. New York: Vintage, 1995. 107–43.

Ferguson, Frances. *Solitude and the Sublime*. New York: Routledge, 1992.

Freud, Sigmund. "The Uncanny." *The Standard Edition of the Complete Psychological Works of Sigmund Freud. Vol. XVII*. Trans. James Strachey. Ed. James Strachey. London: The Hogarth Press, 1955. 217–56.

Fuller, Hoyt. "Towards a Black Aesthetic." Gayle, *The Black Aesthetic*. 3–12.

Gates, Henry Louis, Jr. *Colored People*. New York: Knopf, 1994.

———. "Criticism in the Jungle." *Black Literature and Literary Theory*. Ed Henry Louis Gates, Jr. New York: Methuen, 1984. 1–24.

———. "Preface to Blackness: Text and Pretext." *Within the Circle: An Anthology of African American Literary Criticism from the Harlem Renaissance to the Present*. Ed. Angelyn Mitchell. Durham: Duke University Press, 1994. 235–55.

———. *The Signifying Monkey: A Theory of African-American Literary Criticism*. New York: Oxford University Press, 1988.

———. "Writing 'Race' and the Difference It Makes." *"Race," Writing, and Difference*. Ed. Gates. Chicago: University of Chicago Press, 1986. 1–20.

Gates, Henry Louis, Jr., and Anthony Appiah, eds. *Toni Morrison: Critical Perspectives Past and Present*. New York: Amistad, 1993.

Gayle, Addison, ed.. *The Black Aesthetic*. New York: Doubleday, 1971.

———. "Cultural Strangulation: Black Literature and the White Aesthetic." Gayle, *The Black Aesthetic*. 39–46.

———. "Introduction." Gayle, *The Black Aesthetic*. xv–xxiv.

———. "The Function of Literature at the Present Time." Gayle, *The Black Aesthetic*. 407–19.

Gentry, Marshall Bruce. *Flannery O'Connor's Religion of the Grotesque*. Jackson: University Press of Mississippi, 1986.

Grant, Robert. "Absence into Presence: The Thematics of Memory and 'Missing' Subjects in Toni Morrison's *Sula*." McKay, *Critical Essays on Toni Morrison*. 90–103.

Gross, Linda, and Marian Barnes. *Talk That Talk*. New York: Simon and Schuster, 1989.

Guerrero, Edward. "Tracking 'the look' in the Novels of Toni Morrison." *Black American Literature Forum* 24:4 (1990): 761–64.

Gysin, Fritz. *The Grotesque in American Negro Fiction*. Bern: Francke Verlag, 1975.

Harpham, Geoffrey Galt. *On the Grotesque: Strategies of Contradiction in Art and Literature*. Princeton: Princeton University Press, 1982.

Harris, Middleton, ed. *The Black Book*. New York: Random House, 1974.

Harris, Trudier. *Fiction and Folklore: The Novels of Toni Morrison*. Knoxville: University of Tennessee Press, 1991.

———. "Reconnecting Fragments: Afro-American Folk Tradition in *The Bluest Eye*." McKay, *Critical Essays*. 68–76.

Hassan, Ihab. *The Postmodern Turn: Essays in Postmodern Theory and Culture.* Columbus: Ohio State University Press, 1987.

Heinze, Denise. *The Dilemma of "Double-Consciousness": Toni Morrison's Novels.* Athens: University of Georgia Press, 1993.

Hemenway, Robert. *Zora Neale Hurston: A Literary Biography.* Urbana: University of Illinois Press, 1977.

Hertz, Neil. *The End of the Line: Essays on Psychoanalysis and the Sublime.* New York: Columbia University Press, 1985.

hooks, bell. "From *Black is a Woman's Color.*" *Callaloo* 12:39 (1989): 382–88.

———. "Straightening Our Hair." *Z Magazine* (1988): 14.

Howe, Irving. "Black Boys and Native Sons." *A World More Attractive: A View of Modern Literature and Politics.* New York: Books for Libraries Press, 1963: 98–122.

Hughes, Langston. *The Big Sea.* New York: Hill and Wang, 1963.

———. "The Negro Artist and the Racial Mountain." *Nation* 122 (1928): 692–94.

Hurston, Zora Neale. "How It Feels to be Colored Me." *The World Tomorrow* 11 (1928): 215–16.

———. *Their Eyes Were Watching God.* New York: Harper and Row, 1990.

Jahn, Janheinz. *Muntu: African Culture and the Western World.* New York: Grove Press, 1961.

Jameson, Fredric. *Postmodernism, or, The Cultural Logic of Late Capitalism.* Durham: Duke University Press, 1991.

Jay, Martin. "'The Aesthetic Ideology' as Ideology: Or What Does It Mean to Aestheticize Politics?" *Force Fields: Between Intellectual History and Cultural Critique.* New York: Routledge, 1993. 71–83.

———. *Downcast Eyes: The Denigration of Vision in Twentieth-Century French Thought.* Berkeley: University of California Press, 1993.

Jefferson, Thomas. *The Portable Thomas Jefferson.* Ed. Merrill D. Peterson. New York: Penguin, 1977.

Jones, Bessie W., and Audrey Vinson. "An Interview with Toni Morrison." Taylor-Guthrie 171–87.

Kant, Immanuel. *The Critique of Judgement.* Trans. James Creed Meredith. Oxford: Oxford University Press, 1952.

———. *The Critique of Judgement.* Trans. J. H. Berhard. New York: Hafner, 1951.

Kayser, Wolfgang. *The Grotesque in Art and Literature.* Trans. Ulrich Weisstein. Bloomington: Indiana University Press, 1963.

Keats, John. *The Letters of John Keats.* Ed. Maurice Buxton Forman. Fourth Edition. London: Oxford University Press, 1952.

Kemp, John. *The Philosophy of Kant.* Oxford: Oxford University Press, 1968.

Koenen, Anne. "The One Out of Sequence." Taylor-Guthrie 67–83.

Kolmerton, Carol A., Stephen M. Ross, and Judith Bryant Wittenberg, eds. *Unflinching Gaze: Morrison and Faulkner Re-Envisioned.* Jackson: University Press of Mississippi, 1997.

———. "Introduction: Refusing to Look Away." Kolmerton, *Unflinching Gaze* ix–xv.

Kristeva, Julia. *Desire in Language*. Ed. Leon S. Roudiez. Trans. Thomas Goza, Alice Jardine, and Leon Roudiez. New York: Columbia University Press, 1980.

––––––. "The Ethics of Linguistics." *Modern Criticism and Theory*. Ed. David Lodge. New York: Longman, 1988. 230–39.

Lawrence, David. "Fleshly Ghosts and Ghostly Flesh: The Word and the Body in *Beloved*." *Studies in American Fiction* 19:2 (1991): 189–201.

LeClair, Thomas. "The Language Must Not Sweat: A Conversation with Toni Morrison." Taylor-Guthrie 119–28.

Ledbetter, Mark. *Victims and the Postmodern Narrative or Doing Violence to the Body: An Ethic of Reading and Writing*. New York: St. Martin's, 1996.

Leonard, John. "Her Soul's High Song." Rev. of *Jazz*, by Toni Morrison. *The Nation* 25 May 1992: 706–18.

Leonardo da Vinci. *Treatise on Painting*. Vol. 1 [Codex Urbinas Latinas 1270]. Ed. and Trans. A. P. McMahon. Princeton: Princeton University Press, 1956.

Levine, George, ed. *Aesthetics and Ideology*. New Brunswick: Rutgers University Press, 1994.

––––––. "Introduction: Reclaiming the Aesthetic." Levine, *Aesthetics and Ideology* 1–28.

Lewis, Vaschti Crutcher. "African Tradition in Toni Morrison's *Sula*." *Phylon* 48 (1987): 91–97.

Lyotard, Jean-Francois. "Answering the Question: What Is Postmodernism?" Trans. Regis Durand. *The Postmodern Condition: A Report on Knowledge*. Trans. Geoff Bennington and Brian Massumi. Minneapolis: University of Minnesota Press, 1984. 71–82.

––––––. *The Inhuman: Reflections on Time*. Trans. Geoff Bennington and Rachel Bowlby. Cambridge: Polity Press, 1991.

––––––. "The Interest of the Sublime." *Of the Sublime: Presence in Question*. Ed. Jeffrey Librett. Albany: State University of New York Press, 1993. 109–32.

––––––. *Lessons on the Analytic of the Sublime: Kant's* Critique of Judgement, *sections 23–29*. Stanford: Stanford University Press, 1994.

––––––. "Return Upon the Return." *Toward the Postmodern*. Eds. Robert Harvey and Mark S. Roberts. New Jersey: Humanities Press, 1993.

––––––. "The Sublime and the Avant-Garde." *Paragraph* 6 (1985): 1–18.

Major, Clarence, ed. *Juba to Jive*. New York: Penguin, 1970.

Mason, Theodore O, Jr. "The Novelist as Conservator: Stores and Comprehension in Toni Morrison's *Song of Solomon*." *Contemporary Literature* 29:4 (1988): 564–81.

Mathus, Jill. *Toni Morrison*. Manchester and New York: Manchester University Press, 1998.

Mbalia, Doreatha Drummond. "Women Who Run with Wild: The Need for Sisterhoods in *Jazz*." *Modern Fiction Studies* 39:3–4 (1993): 623–50.

McDowell, Deborah. "'The Self and the Other': Reading Toni Morrison's *Sula* and the Black Female Text." McKay, *Critical Essays* 77–90.

McElroy, Bernard. *Fiction of the Modern Grotesque*. London: Macmillan, 1989.

McKay, Nellie. "An Interview with Toni Morrison." Taylor-Guthrie 138–55.

———, ed. *Critical Essays on Toni Morrison.* Boston: G. K. Hall, 1988.

———. "Introduction." McKay, *Critical Essays* 1–15.

Merleau-Ponty, M. *Phenomenology of Perception.* Trans. Colin Smith. London and New York: Routledge and Kegan Paul, 1962.

Minor, Madonne M. "Lady No Longer Sings the Blues: Rape, Madness, and Silence in *The Bluest Eye.*" *Toni Morrison.* Ed. Harold Bloom. New York: Chelsea House, 1986. 85–99.

Monk, Samuel. *The Sublime: A Study of Critical Theories in Eighteenth-Century England.* New York: Modern Languages Association, 1935.

Morrison, Toni. "Afterword." *The Bluest Eye.* New York: Penguin, 1994. 209–16.

———. "Behind the Making of *The Black Book.*" *Black World* February 1974: 86–90.

———. *Beloved.* New York: Alfred A. Knopf, 1987.

———. *The Bluest Eye.* New York: Simon and Schuster, 1970.

———. "City Limits, Village Values: Concepts of the Neighborhood in Black Fiction." *Literature and the Urban Experience: Essays on the City and Literature.* Eds. Michael C. Jaye and Ann Chalmers Watts. New Brunswick: Rutgers University Press, 1981. 35–43.

———. *The Dancing Mind: Speech Upon Acceptance of the National Book Foundation Medal for Distinguished Contribution to American Letters, on the Sixth of November, Nineteen Hundred and Ninety-Six.* New York: Alfred A. Knopf, 1997.

———. *Jazz.* New York: Alfred A. Knopf, 1992.

———. "Memory, Creation, Writing." *Thought* 59 (1984): 385–90.

———. "Mercy." *Four Songs* set for soprano, cello, and piano by Andre Previn. Performed by Sylvia McNair, Yo-Yo Ma, and Previn. *From Ordinary Things,* Sony Classical compact disc, 1997.

———. *The Nobel Lecture.* New York: Norton, 1993.

———. *Paradise.* New York: Alfred A. Knopf, 1998.

———. *Playing in the Dark: Whiteness and the Literary Imagination.* Cambridge: Harvard University Press, 1992.

———. "Preface." Toni Cade Bambara. *Deep Sightings and Rescue Missions.* New York: Pantheon. vii–xi.

———. Rev. of *Amisted 2, New African Literature and the Arts,* and *The Black Aesthetic. New York Times Book Review* 28 February 1971: 5, 34.

———. *Song of Solomon.* New York: Penguin, 1987.

———. *Sula.* New York: Penguin, 1973.

———. *Tar Baby.* New York: Penguin, 1982.

———. "Unspeakable Things Unspoken: The Afro-American Presence in American Literature." *Michigan Quarterly Review* 28 (1989): 1–34.

———. "Virginia Woolf's and William Faulkner's Treatment of the Alienated." Thesis. Cornell University, 1955.

———. "What the Black Woman Thinks About Women's Lib." *The New York Times Magazine,* 22 August 1971: 14–15, 63–66.

Moyers, Bill. "A Conversation with Toni Morrison." Taylor-Guthrie 262–74.

Naylor, Gloria. "A Conversation: Gloria Naylor and Toni Morrison." Taylor-Guthrie 188–217.

Neal, Larry. "The Black Arts Movement." Gayle, *The Black Aesthetic*. 272–90.

O'Connor, Flannery. "Some Aspects of the Grotesque in Southern Fiction." *Mystery and Manners: Occasional Prose*. Eds. Sally Fitzgerald and Robert Fitzgerald. New York: Farrar, 1969. 36–50.

O'Meally, Robert. "Ralph Ellison." *American Writers: A Collection of Literary Biographies. Supplement II, Part 1*. Ed. in Chief, A. Walton Litz. New York: Charles Scribner's and Sons, 1981. 221–52.

———. "Tar Baby, She Don' Say Nothin.'" McKay, *Critical Essays*. 33–37.

O'Shaugnessy, Kathleen. "'Life life life life': The Community as Chorus in *Song of Solomon*." McKay, *Critical Essays*. 125–33.

Page, Philip. *Dangerous Freedom: Fusion and Fragmentation in Toni Morrison's Novels*. Jackson: University Press of Mississippi, 1995.

Paris, Peter. *The Spirituality of African Peoples: The Search for a Common Moral Discourse*. Minneapolis: Fortress, 1995.

Peiss, Kathy. "Making Faces: The Cosmetic Industry and the Cultural Construction of Gender 1890–1930." *Genders* 7 (1990): 143–69.

———. *Hope in a Jar: The Making of America's Beauty Culture*. New York: Metropolitan Books/Henry Holt, 1998.

Peterson, Nancy. "Introduction: Reading Toni Morrison—From the Seventies to the Nineties." *Toni Morrison: Critical and Theoretical Approaches*. Ed. Nancy Peterson. Baltimore: Johns Hopkins University Press, 1997: 1–15.

———. "'Say make me, remake me': Toni Morrison and the Reconstruction of African-American History." *Toni Morrison: Critical and Theoretical Approaches*. Ed. Nancy Peterson. Baltimore: Johns Hopkins University Press, 1997: 201–21.

Petry, Ann. *The Street*. New York: Pyramid Books, 1973.

Porter, Gladys L. *Three Negro Pioneers in Beauty Culture*. New York: Vintage, 1966.

Potter, Eliza. *A Hairdresser's Experience in High Life*[1859]. New York: Oxford University Press, 1991.

Powell, T. B. "Toni Morrison: The Struggle to Depict the Black Figure on the White Page." *Black American Literature Forum* (1990): 747–60.

Proust, Marcel. *Remembrance of Things Past*. Trans. C. K. Scott Moncrieff, Terence Kilmartin, and Andres Mayor. New York: Random House, 1980.

Rampersad, Arnold. *The Life of Langston Hughes, Volume I: 1902–1941: I, Too, Sing America*. New York: Oxford University Press, 1986.

———. *The Life of Langston Hughes, Volume II: 1941–1967: I Dream a World*. New York: Oxford University Press, 1988.

Rigney, Barbara Hill. *The Voices of Toni Morrison*. Columbus: Ohio State University Press, 1991.

Rooks, Noliwe M. *Hair Raising: Beauty, Culture, and African American Women*. New Brunswick: Rutgers University Press, 1996.

Rorty, Richard. "Cosmopolitanism without Emancipation: A Response to Jean-Francois Lyotard." *Objectivity, Relativism, Truth: Philosophical Papers, Volume I*. Cambridge: Cambridge University Press, 1991. 211–22.

———. "Habermas and Lyotard on Postmodernity." *Essays on Heidegger and Others: Philosophical Papers, Volume II*. Cambridge: Cambridge University Press, 1991. 164–76.

Rosenberg, Ruth. "Seeds in Hard Ground: Black Girlhood in *The Bluest Eye*." *Black American Literature Forum* 21:4 (1987): 435–45.

Ruas, Charles. "Toni Morrison." Taylor-Guthrie 93–118.

Rushdie, Salman. *Shame*. London: Vintage, 1995.

———. *The Moor's Last Sigh*. New York: Random House, 1995.

Rushing, Andrea Benton. "Hair Raising." *Feminist Studies* 14:2 (1988): 325–35.

Russo, Mary J. *The Female Grotesque: Risk, Excess and Modernity*. New York and London: Routledge, 1994.

Sale, Maggie. "Call and Response as Critical Method." *African American Review* 26:1 (1992): 41–50.

Scarry, Elaine. *On Beauty and Being Just*. Princeton: Princeton University Press, 1999.

Schapiro, Barbara. "The Bonds of Love and the Boundaries of Self in Toni Morrison's *Beloved*." *Contemporary Literature* 32:2 (1991): 194–210.

Smith, Barbara. "Toward a Black Feminist Criticism." *All the Women Are White, All the Blacks Are Men, But Some of Us Are Brave*. Eds. Gloria T. Hull, Patricia Bell Scott, and Barbara Smith. Old Westbury, New York: Feminist Press, 1982. 157–75.

Smith, Valerie. *Self-Discovery and Authority in Afro-American Narrative*. Cambridge: Harvard University Press, 1987.

Smitherman, Geneva. *Talkin and Testifyin*. Detroit: Wayne State University Press, 1977.

———. *Black Talk*. New York: Houghton Mifflin, 1994.

Somerville, Jane. "Idealized Beauty and the Denial of Love in Toni Morrison's *The Bluest Eye*." *Bulletin of the West Virginia Association of College English Teachers* 9:1 (1986): 18–23.

Stein, K. F. "Toni Morrison's Sula: A Black Woman's Epic." *Black American Literature Forum* 21 (1987): 146–50.

Stendhal. *Love*. Trans. Gilbert and Suzanne Sele. Middlesex: Penguin, 1975.

Stepto, Robert B. "Intimate Things in Place: A Conversation with Toni Morrison." Taylor-Guthrie 10–29.

———. "The Reconstruction of Instruction." *Afro-American Literature: The Reconstruction of Instruction*. Eds. Dexter Fisher and Robert B. Stepto. New York: Modern Languages Association, 1979. 8–24.

Storace, Patricia. "The Scripture of Utopia." Rev. of *Paradise*, by Toni Morrison. *The New York Review of Books* 11 June 1998: 64–69.

Summers, David. *The Judgement of Sense: Renaissance Naturalism and the Rise of Aesthetics*. Cambridge: Cambridge University Press, 1987.

Tate, Claudia. "Toni Morrison." Taylor-Guthrie 156–70.

Taylor-Guthrie, Danille, ed. *Conversations with Toni Morrison.* Jackson: University Press of Mississippi, 1994.

"This Side of Paradise." Rev. of *Paradise*, by Toni Morrison. Amazon.Com (1998). N.p. Online. Internet. Available: amazon.com.

Trace, Jacqueline. "Dark Goddesses: Black Feminist Theology in Morrison's *Beloved.*" *Obsidian II* 6 (1991): 14–30. \

Wall, Cheryl. "On Freedom and the Will to Adorn: Debating Aesthetics and/as Ideology in African-American Literature." Levine, *Aesthetics and Ideology*. 283–303.

Wallace, Michele. "If You Can't Join 'Em, Beat 'Em." *Transition: An International Review* 51 (1991): 214–25.

Walling, William. "'Art' and 'Protest': Ralph Ellison's *Invisible Man* Twenty Years After." *Phylon* 34 (1973): 120–34.

Walther, Malin LaVon. "Out of Sight: Toni Morrison's Revision of Beauty." *Black American Literature Forum* 24:4 (1990): 775–90.

Washington, Booker T. *Working with the Hands.* New York: Doubleday, Page and Co., 1904.

Watkins, Mel. "Talk with Toni Morrison." Taylor-Guthrie 43–47.

Washington, Elsie. "Talk with Toni Morrison." Taylor-Guthrie 234–38.

Washington, Mary Helen. "A Woman Half in Shadow." *Modern Critical Views: Zora Neale Hurston.* Ed. Harold Bloom. New York: Chelsea, 1986: 123–38.

Weems, Renita. "'Artists without art form': A Look at One Black Woman's World of Unrevered Black Women." *Home Girls: A Black Feminist Anthology.* Ed. Barbara Smith. New York: Kitchen Table: Women of Color Press, 1983. 94–105.

Wegs, Joyce. "Toni Morrison's *Song of Solomon*: A Blues Song." *Essays in Literature* 9 (1982): 211–23.

Weiskel, Thomas. *The Romantic Sublime: Studies in the Structure and Psychology of Transcendence.* Baltimore: Johns Hopkins University Press, 1976.

Williams, Raymond. *Keywords: A Vocabulary of Culture and Society.* New York: Oxford University Press, 1976.

Wilson, Judith. "A Conversation with Toni Morrison." Taylor-Guthrie 129–37.

Wood, James. *The Broken Estate: Essays on Literature and Belief.* London: Jonathan Cape, 1999.

Wright, Richard. "Blueprint for Negro Writing." *New Challenge* 2 (1937): 53–65.

———. "Between Laughter and Tears." *New Masses* 5 Oct. 1937.

CONTRIBUTORS

Yvonne Atkinson is a lecturer at California State University, San Bernardino, and a doctoral candidate at the University of California, Riverside. She has published essays on Toni Morrison, the oral tradition of Black English, and Frederick Douglass. Her dissertation, "The Mammy Figure in American Literature and Popular Culture," will be completed in December 2000.

Marc C. Conner is an assistant professor in the English Department at Washington and Lee University. He has published essays on Toni Morrison, Thomas Pynchon, Salman Rushdie, and Sherwood Anderson, and is completing a book examining the aesthetics of the sublime and the beautiful in the twentieth-century American novel.

Susan Corey is an associate professor of English at California Lutheran University. She has published essays on Toni Morrison and has co-edited two collections of American diaries and letters: *The American Journey: U.S. History in Letters and Diaries*, volumes I and II, and *Writing Women's Lives: American Women's History in Letters and Diaries*.

Maria DiBattista is a professor of English and comparative literature at Princeton University, where she teaches modern literature and film. She is the author of *First Love: The Affections of Modern Fiction* (Chicago, 1991), and *Virginia Woolf's Major Novels: The Fables of Anon* (Yale, 1979), and co-editor, with Lucy McDiarmid, of *High and Low Moderns* (Oxford, 1997). She has just completed *Fast-Talking Dames*, a book on women and screwball comedy, and is at work on a study of the novels of sentimental education.

Barbara Johnson is professor of English and American literature and language at Harvard University. She is the author of a number of books, including *The Feminist Dif-*

ference: *Literature, Psychoanalysis, Race, and Gender* (Harvard, 1998), *The Wake of Deconstruction* (Blackwell, 1994), *A World of Difference* (Johns Hopkins, 1987), and *The Critical Difference: Essays in the Contemporary Rhetoric of Reading* (Johns Hopkins, 1980).

Cheryl Lester is an associate professor of English and American studies at the University of Kansas. She has published essays on critical theory, William Faulkner, Black Migration, and Elvis Presley, and is completing a book on Faulkner and the Great Migration that is forthcoming from Cambridge University Press.

Katherine Stern is director of Advocacy and Education for Cultural Survival, an indigenous peoples' rights organization. She received her doctorate in comparative literature from Princeton University, and was an assistant professor at the University of Alaska, Fairbanks, and a junior fellow at the Harvard Society of Fellows. She has published articles on suffragette-era fantasy literature and on "What is Femme: The Phenomenology of the Powder Room." She is currently completing a book titled, *Men in Makeup: Wilde, Mann, and Proust on the Problem of Male Metamorphosis*.

Michael Wood is Charles Barnwell Stuart Professor of English at Princeton University, and the author of books on Stendhal, García Márquez, and Nabokov. His most recent work is *Children of Silence: On Contemporary Fiction* (Columbia, 1998). He writes frequently on literature and film for the *New York Review of Books* and the *London Review of Books*, and a number of other journals.

Index

1488